UNDER SAIL

UNDER SAIL

BBC PUBLICATIONS

This book is dedicated to Brian Hawkins, producer of the BBC2
television series *Under Sail*, whose enthusiasm has been
an essential contribution to the book.

Published by BBC Publications,
a division of BBC Enterprises Ltd,
35 Marylebone High Street, London w1M 4AA

First published 1986

ISBN 0 563 20493 1

Typeset in 11/13 Imprint by Phoenix Photosetting, Chatham
Printed in England by Mackays of Chatham Ltd
Cover printed by Belmont Press Ltd

CONTENTS

INTRODUCTION

To sail the sea is to embrace a seamless strand of history; and one of the more pleasing aspects of the final decades of this technological century is that the same beings who walked the moon still find an irresistible challenge in the oceans of the world, and a beguiling pleasure in its coastal waters and riverways. However many years have come and gone, the sensing of the wind and the harnessing of it, and the sheer skill and joy of the perfect setting of sails, continues unchanged. The romantic attraction has never lessened. It is as if, in an age of fact, we have an even greater need of poetry – and poetry is part of every sailing boat that ever put to sea.

In the beginning, of course, sail was the key that unlocked the world. Today, it is hardly that; but the mastery of sail still represents a challenge like no other. It requires a coming to terms with Nature, and the modern sailors – on barques and brigantines or crabbing off West Country coasts or assessing the tides and winds of lasting estuaries – are of the same breed as those of old who had little else to keep themselves alive save hoisting a rag of a sail.

The wonder is that, for all the twentieth century has given us in its inventiveness, the meeting of sail and wind has, almost alone of its age, survived. You can see it, even today, precisely as you could have seen it centuries ago. Step on to any sailing boat – a restored square-rigger, where above you there will be an area of sail to equal the span of a football pitch; an estuary dinghy, with its tiny, flapping sails; a working boat in a Cornish creek; or a splendid black barge on the Thames, or among the reeds in a Norfolk landscape – and what you will realise, above all else, is that little has changed; that sailing folk and Nature *expect* to meet and that, together, they seem to find a unique mutual respect.

Despite the fact that these days, except in leisure and competitive sailing, the whole concept of sail tends to be surrounded by a sense of old-fashionedness, the truth is that not much above a mere half-century ago, a great deal of the world's trade was still conducted under sail.

During the Second World War, of course, and in the decade after it, the whole of that era virtually vanished, and many of the magnificent ships which had served us well lay useless and rotting on beaches and moorings around the world. A few were saved and lovingly restored and, as time went on, others were built in their image. There was a longing and also a determination that while years inevitably passed away, it did not follow that all that graced them should surrender – and sail, in a way, refused to die. Indeed, it took on a new life.

Great navigators such as Sir Francis Chichester saw in sail one of the few remaining challenges left to people destined to live in an age increasingly dominated by the machine, and the roll of those like him, who saw sail as an adventure, grew. As for leisure sailing, it became more popular than it had ever been. New classes of boats were designed and marinas built to accommodate them; estuary moorings proliferated; and boat builders, while regretful at the passing of timber as the one essential element of their craft, turned to plastics and moulds which became just as sustaining to their honourable trade. The result has been that, far from the inshore waters of Britain being denuded of sail, they became coloured by the most glorious of hues: huge billowing spinnakers of red, blue, green and gold, a growing fleet of tiny yachts.

Alongside it all, too, new wooden boats were built, and old wooden ones restored, with powered winches and shrouds of stainless-steel wire, and they were sailed with a new sort of pleasure that their earlier years could scarcely have allowed. In Danish and Finnish yards and in Britain and farther south, barques and brigantines and schooners were built to give opportunities to young people, in sail-training enterprises, to experience the sort of demands that ships of their like had always placed on those who sailed them, thereby making them better people.

It is in all these areas that the makers of the BBC television series *Under Sail* have worked, and they have produced programmes of appeal to an audience far larger, I suspect, than was once thought likely. Such success is undoubtedly due, in no small measure, to the care and enthusiasm that goes into every *Under Sail* production, and this derives totally from the two producers who have charted its course. Robin Drake (who, sadly, died recently) and Brian Hawkins – what appropriate surnames for men producing sailing programmes – working out of the BBC's Network Production Centre in Bristol, have gathered around themselves a tiny but talented team of young directors and cameramen to realise their ideas.

Sitting in my narrator's box and listening over my headphones to the talk in the production gallery, I never ceased to be both thankful for, and impressed by, the wishes and the skills that surrounded me.

There is also a second reason for the series' success, which I think cannot be underestimated. *Under Sail* touches a chord in the British character which will never fade; addresses itself to a people who, throughout the whole of their history, have depended on the sea and who, even today, think more often of sail than of super-tankers.

When the idea for *Under Sail* was first born, the force of the argument for such a series was no doubt buttressed by the notion 'If we don't capture this sort of material now, it will be lost forever'. In the event, however, while the series' producers may have honestly thought that what they wanted to do would imprison history, they found, to their delight, that they could turn their cameras upon a celebration of a continuing story – a story which gives every indication of being endless. The *Under Sail* production team is in the happy position of not having to worry about what to film next but rather what to delay. There is so much more waiting to be reflected.

A few years ago, I was talking to Alan Villiers, who sailed in square-riggers with a cine-camera when young and who later took the marvellous replica of the *Mayflower* across the Atlantic. We were talking about a yachtsman who had just made banner headlines for rounding the Horn. I shall never forget what he said: 'Guys are doing it all the time. They end up on the beach for a while, and then they start off again. Sail! Mark my words, sail started it, and sail will be there if the end ever comes.'

As for the contributors to this book, they share the precepts that *Under Sail* has set itself. Here they write on their own special subjects, but with a common bond: a love of sail. If there is a difference, it is purely one of scale.

John Hamilton, Race Director of the Sail Training Association, writes of the work of an organisation which has done much to show young people aspects of times now gone which could be helpful today; Peter Ferguson, the originator and editor of *Topsail*, considers those wonderful Thames barges from the standpoint of a man who, as a young boy, stood on the coastline of Somerset within sight of the last of the trading ketches and schooners working the Bristol Channel ports.

Ian Dear, who has written extensively on yachting, selects a subject much more glamorous – the story of the J-class yachts: an evocation of an era when these superb craft and their attempts on the America's Cup stamped themselves across their times as vividly as the jazz music so often played on gramophones in their crew quarters. Robert Simper, a member of the Society for Nautical Research and President of the Old Gaffers Association, is a prolific writer on traditional sailing ships – primarily aiming to encourage people to restore old boats. (He himself owns a 35-foot gaff cutter built in 1904, and he is currently restoring an 1896 beach boat.)

Jack Coote writes on competition in one-designs, the sort of racing that so excitingly fills the summer yachting calendar around our coasts. He is an experienced cruising yachtsman who also possesses a quite extensive library of sailing books which, among other things, helped him to compile his *Down the Wind*, a much acclaimed anthology of sailing literature; and Dr Leslie Morrish, a consultant psychiatrist, medical director, and senior lecturer at the University of London, writes affectionately of the West Country trading ketch *Irene* which he has caringly restored and which, one of these days, he hopes to sail around the world.

All these contributors write out of a comprehensive knowledge of their chosen subjects; the two chapters that I contribute rely totally on the knowledge of others. For one, I have called upon the memories of some of the oyster fishermen of the River Fal in Cornwall; and for the other upon the recollections of a single man, Mr A. J. Pengelly, one of Cornwall's most respected sea fishermen. I am grateful for the time they spared me and the help they gave.

This book sets out to encompass, in a more lasting and leisurely fashion than can television, some parts of the story that *Under Sail* has sought to reflect. It is a story well worth the remembering and the telling. For no nation has relished the sea more than ours, nor sailed our nearer waters nor wider ones with more pleasure, need or bravery. For us to ignore the sea, and the sail that took us upon it, would be like ignoring the land upon which we live. That sail should linger ought to surprise no one; that it should be disregarded would be the only puzzle.

Tom Salmon
Cornwall, April 1986

1
THE OYSTERMEN OF THE FAL
Tom Salmon

You can see these small, sturdy working boats, far fewer now than they once were, dawdling just below the gentle hills that surround the tideway of the River Fal and funnel its estuary into a mysterious mixture of cosy rivers. In autumn, winter and spring they are there, when for the most part the tourists have gone and Cornwall returns to a life not much changed down the years, and the Cornish set about work that their fathers and grandfathers and great-grandfathers have always done. And you will see them, if you're a discerning visitor, on summer weekends when they race.

The beautiful Falmouth working boats are a real fragment of Cornish history. These small gaff-rigged cutters, dredging for oysters by a method little changed for centuries, are the only sailing boats in Western Europe still in commercial use. Built cheaply for poor fishermen, often on the open foreshore, in their modest fashion they are as perfect in design for the work they do as any sailing vessel that ever came from a boatyard. Slow and stable enough to drift with the tide while dredging, they must also be able to get up a good speed to dash back to their starting point to squeeze in another drift – slow on the first course, fast on the second.

Oyster boats were generally built in one of two sizes. A 28-footer, meant for two men, could work four dredges; a one-man boat, about 23 feet long, worked two. The draught was never more than 4 or 5 feet, and in other ways the boats are all much the same: forward, they have a small fo'c'sle used for stowing gear, but the rest of the craft is little more than an open cockpit.

The four dredges of the larger boat are precisely placed. One is just aft of the shrouds, another amidships on the weather side, the third on the quarter and the fourth over the stern. Usually one man works the two forward ones and the other the two after ones, although even today there is one young man much admired on the Fal – the Cornish have a

Opposite: *Dolly*, **a working boat built in 1914, in the 1980 Greenbank Race**

strong regard for physical prowess – who can work three dredges alone.

One of the reasons the boats are so well suited to their job is the gaff rig. Any oysterman will tell you that there's no rig more adaptable: you can drop the peak halliards, trice up the boom, and let go of the storm jibs that can turn a gale into a breeze. In many ways, the regard of oystermen for their working boats is a love affair, and it is a relationship that has stood the test of time.

The Fal oyster industry is thousands of years old. There is evidence that the Romans dredged for oysters in the river, and it is believed that the industry has continued, on and off, since that time.

Of all the boats that have fished the oyster banks, perhaps the most venerable is the *Morning Star*. When she was built, no one is quite sure,

Below: Frank Cock, skipper of the *Morning Star*

but when Frank Cock bought her in 1949 she was said to be 136 years of age. That puts her launch at 1813, yet Mr Cock and his partner were still sailing her for oyster fishing in 1980.

She was built, or so her legendary history goes, as a pilchard drifter, working out of Portloe on Cornwall's fish-rich southern coast. Twenty-six feet long (later extended by 8 feet) and 10 feet in the beam, she has a draught of 5 feet – ideal for oyster fishing. And that was how she was used, until one night in 1980 when she was rammed at her moorings in Restronguet Creek. Frank Cock woke up to look at her, as he always did, from the bedroom window of his cottage and saw only the tip of her mast. 'It was one of the saddest days of my life,' he says.

Frank Cock, eighty now, still looks over the oyster banks that he and his father before him fished. It was a life he loved, and as he talks you can see that, as much as the fishing, he relished the racing back under sail to begin another dredge. If he has a remaining wish, it is that *Morning Star* may yet be restored and that he might sail in her once again. At the moment, she lies in a local boatyard – she was thought, after her sinking, to be a danger to navigation, so she was refloated with air-bags and towed there – and there has been talk on and off about her restoration. It would indeed be sad if this piece of our sailing industry were lost forever.

As for Frank Cock, he first sailed the banks with his father in the early 1920s, but after two seasons – as so often it has down the years – the oyster trade declined, and Frank's father thought it prudent for his son to learn a trade. So Frank became a shipwright like many other oyster-men and more than once rowed to work, 4 miles to Falmouth Docks. However, the two seasons he had spent on the banks never faded from his mind and, having bought *Morning Star* with a partner for a mere £250, he returned to them.

Little, he found, had changed. You bought a licence for each dredge, and you also bought a brass ring 2⅝ inches in diameter. If any oyster you dredged went through this ring, you were obliged to return it to the sea – 'Or', as Frank now wryly recalls, 'you were *supposed* to.' But if you did not, there was always the possibility that the oyster bailiff might come alongside you, and you could end up before the magistrates.

For well-nigh thirty years Frank Cock worked the oyster banks of the Fal: to make a half-year's living, to be sure, but also to be among men who shared a special subtlety of sailing. There were good times and bad. In the mid-1950s, for example, the local newspapers reported a yield of '3,500,000 oysters which have supplied leading hotels all over the country', and they recalled that 'in recent years a box of Fal oysters was among the birthday gifts to the Prime Minister, Sir Winston Churchill.'

At that time, there were sixty and more dredgermen 'finding a remunerative occupation in the industry', but even the euphoric writings of local journalists never disguised the reality of what has always been, at best, a tenuous trade. 'They are fishermen-farmers most of them, for all their sailing skills; and they need orchards or small-holdings to augment their incomes.'

Thus it had ever been, even in the heyday of the Fal oyster fishery. The sailing skills of the oystermen, part-time or not, were always hard to rival. Before the War they spent their summers crewing the fabulous J-class yachts or working the thriving schooner coastal trade. But their first love nonetheless remained working the oyster banks.

The dredging technique used by the Falmouth oystermen is decep-tively simple. While the boat is allowed to drift with the tide, following the twists and turns along one of the three oyster banks, the dredges are dragged behind. They must be hauled in and emptied constantly through the drift. When the end of the bank is reached, the boat is sailed quickly back to start again. The dredgerman has to have an exact 'map' of the bank in his head and detailed knowledge of the depth of water at any given point. He must be able to drift at exactly the right speed – achieved by raising or lowering the mainsail – taking into account both wind and tide. If too slow, he will pick up more mud than oysters, and if too fast he will skip over most of them. The dredgermen say it takes ten years to become really skilful.

There was once a yachtsman, so the story goes, who sailed the Carrick Roads of the Fal so sublimely one summer that he thought he would stay on for the winter. To make a little money to sustain himself, he reckoned that oyster dredging would suit. He was a splendid sailor; his yacht (bermudan-rigged, classy and expensive) had done well in summer racing; and he thought the winter oyster living would be easy. So one night he turned up in the Mylor Yacht Club and fell among one or two who were knowledgeable in the ways of the oyster fishery.

'I have a mind', he said, 'to stay over the winter and fish for oysters.'

'Really?' they asked. 'And what boat are you going to use?'

'Mine,' he answered.

'Yours?' they queried. 'No chance.'

Nevertheless he stayed on and tried it, but after a fortnight he gave up. To this day, the oystermen remember him: sailing in a boat ten

Above: Winter on the Fal in the good years of the 1950s

times more sophisticated and expensive than theirs, but not fashioned for the work at hand – a simple enough job, yet dependent totally on skills and boats that owe everything to years of experience.

Today, the days of many of the Falmouth fleet of oyster boats are marked more by pleasure than by work. In lingering Cornish summers along the Fal, the oyster boats grace weekend regattas with a style and elegance of sailing and skill which might seem surprising in a working boat. Whether the boats are *pretty* or not is a matter of opinion, but when racing they certainly strike the observer as handsome: they dash along, their bows rising straight from the water, swerving with speed and skill around cunningly set marker buoys to the finishing line.

There was a time – between the Wars, certainly – when all these boats would have been sailed exclusively by the oystermen themselves. A few still are, and the names of the crewmen are just the same as they would have been then. Over the years, however, the fishery has declined – never more dramatically than in recent years. A crippling disease caused by a blood parasite called Bonamia, having all but wiped out many of the finest oyster stocks in Europe, has spread to the Fal. There are more boats now than the industry can sustain, and many are used solely for pleasure by summertime sailors who see in their design a manoeuvrability and performance perfectly suited to estuary racing. This is hardly surprising, for though the oyster boats may seem sluggish as they tow their dredges, when they turn to go back to begin another dredging run they put up a spread of sail which seems wildly out of proportion to their size and cut through the sea like racing yachts.

There has been another change, too, in the Falmouth working boat. In the regattas between the Wars, all the boats were made of wood, but now no longer. One or two, even quite recently, still are, but the majority are made of glass-reinforced plastic. It is not that the carpentry skills of the old builders have entirely disappeared; they have not. But the newer material works out much cheaper.

For all the reduction of the oyster-dredging fleet, however, the love of the boats that fished the banks has never been deeper; nor, in some strange way, has the feeling for the fishery been more profound. Yet you will never find an oysterman who believes his son could have a lasting future in it. 'I've seen the best of it, me 'ansum,' they are much more likely to say. ''Tidden what it was.'

Still, even when the oyster fishing was good, it was a hard life. The old oystermen – most of them elderly men, now in their seventies or even eighties – do not recall it with a rosy glow. As the fingers of the farmers froze in the fields above them, so did theirs freeze as they harvested their own crop. And, like the farmers, who wondered from time to time why their prices were so low when the shop prices were so high, the oystermen asked why what they received for their shellfish fell so far short of what the gourmets paid in warm and cosy restaurants. Yet it is clear that they feel a deep pride in the skills they so naturally inherited, and a kind of passion for a job which, although tough, called for qualities they felt themselves fortunate to possess and be able to use.

The building of a wooden Falmouth working boat, or a Truro river oyster dredger, as they were called in the old days, could take a creekside builder many months. In part, the time was needed to ensure that the finished vessel would be the equal of (or superior to) any other boat out on the banks. Today, proof of this persists. There are boats launched a century or so ago which are still under sail and as good now as they ever were.

The fishermen's tradition of naming boats after members of their families threads itself through the fleet: the *Evelyn* and the *Katrina*, the *Magdalena*, the *Stella* and the *Muriel*. Just as lasting are the names of the boats' builders – the Ferrises and the Hitchens and the Heards, men who are as much a part of this lingering industry as the men who fish it.

Not all the boats which have fished the oyster banks, however, were specifically designed for them. To the layman many would have looked the same – yet in one particular they were quite right. The gaff rig, so perfect for dredging, is common to all, and the shape of the hull hardly differs, but the true oyster dredger has the shallowest of draughts: anything over 5 feet was frowned upon. The perfect length for a two-man boat scarcely ever exceeded 28 feet, and the builders of the best of them, who worked purely 'by eye' and without plans, invariably bore this in mind.

The oyster fishery of Cornwall is not the only Cornish fishing industry to have faced the vagaries of what has always been a gambling trade, and occasionally traditional offshore Cornish fishing boats were adapted to oyster dredging. The *Mildred* is such a boat. Built originally in 1912 by R. D. Pill at Gorran Haven for the mackerel fishery, at 28 feet, she was just right for the oyster banks. Her draught was a touch deep, but she was sailed for a decade or so with no small degree of success by a man whose previous sailing experience had been in square-riggers around the Horn and schooners in eastern waters.

Before that, in the 1930s, the *Mildred* had belonged to the novelist Howard Spring, who then lived in Mylor. He gave her perhaps the best assessment ever made of an essentially working boat: 'She's no fancy piece,' he wrote, 'no rich man's mistress. She's a worker, and not a plaything.' Although Spring was not writing of a true oyster boat, she was as near to one as makes scarcely any difference; and indeed one of her subsequent owners proved the point when he sailed her for years over the banks.

What Spring had seen as a novelist, and enjoyed as a sailor, was the very essence of the Falmouth working-boat fleet. The vessels have a practicality that is much to be admired, but also possess other qualities that can be teased from them by true men of the sea, whether sailing for work or for pleasure.

For the most part, the Falmouth oyster boats work mostly in the Carrick Roads these days – at least, the sailing boats do. Further up the Fal, in placid little creeks, oysters are still dredged (though in much reduced numbers) by punt fishermen. In these craft the men stand to their oars and look ahead, rather than sitting and looking over their shoulders – a rowing style that watermen in Falmouth harbour still use.

The Carrick Roads lie just inside the vast sweep of Falmouth Bay, one of the largest natural harbours in the world. It is a spread of sea so big that when Richard Carew, that most observant of Cornish historians, saw it four centuries ago, he wrote, 'Falmouth braggeth that a hundred sail may anchor within its circuit, and not one of these sees the other's top.' Just inside, past today's docks and St Mawes (where there were also once oyster banks), the dredgermen work. The longest bank runs for a couple of miles past the beautifully named St Just-in-Roseland; the smaller ones lie off places such as Mylor and Restronguet.

The oyster-dredging season is both constant and precise. It lasts from the beginning of October to the end of March, from nine in the morning to three in the afternoon, with a half day on Saturday and a complete day's rest on Sunday – and every fifth of November. For the oystermen of the Fal, November 5th has wider connotations than the backyard bonfires of the rest of Britain, for on that day, many years ago now, they fought a battle of principle that took them to the highest court of the land – and won.

Anyone who knows the Cornish will be aware that they are inordinately distrustful of foreign justice – and by 'foreign' the Cornish invariably mean any assembly of judges who happen to sit on the wrong side of the Tamar. But so great was the wrath of the oystermen, and so aggrieved did they feel, that they petitioned the High Court itself, for what was at stake for them was no less than their livelihood.

For as long as they could remember, the oystermen had always put their daily catches between the tide-marks of the beaches near their homes. In those days they couldn't sell their oysters easily: there were no local merchants, and the fishermen had to wait until the French turned up to haggle over the catch. In the meantime the oysters, unless periodically washed by the tide, would have gone bad. For many years the tide-washing of catches had been accepted. More than that, it was absolutely vital to the welfare of the industry. One day, however, someone came along and said that the oystermen were using the foreshore illegally. From that moment the battle was joined. Lawyers and barristers became involved and it all took a long time, but in the end the oystermen won. The exact date of this great victory is uncertain, but it must have been before the First World War.

For the oystermen, the decision was crucial to the continuance of their tiny industry, and they celebrate it even now in the way such victories are traditionally celebrated: they take the day off. On this day, instead of dredging, they race each other, matching the sailing skills that even at work mark one oyster fisherman from another. For all the competition of the summer regattas, the Silver Oyster Race is the 'Derby' of the oystermen's racing calendar – racing is restricted to oystermen only, the prizes are silver replicas of oyster shells, and the sails are precisely the 'working' sails of the oyster banks.

Below: *Agnes* (with ferro-cement hull), second in the 1985 Silver Oyster Race

The fishing hours of the oyster fleet are rigidly controlled, not just by tradition but by local by-laws, drawn up between the Wars with the approval of the oyster fishermen themselves. There are really only two ways of controlling a fishery which has a finite life: one is to impose quotas (but fishermen and quotas have seldom been easy bedfellows), and the other is to limit the amount of fishing that can be undertaken. The oystermen of the Fal chose the second option – as much as anything, one suspects, to underline the view that they have held for centuries that, within a given time, the chances are that the best and most skilful will, in the end, be best rewarded. The local council backed their decision. They also banned the use of motorised vessels, thereby helping to preserve a centuries-old tradition of sail.

On the face of it, the life may seem easy. But, of course, the working day is much longer than these rules might imply – as one oysterman's description of the start of a typical day shows:

> You get out early in the morning, and your dredger will be on moorings off Mylor or Flushing, say. The first thing you do is to see where the wind is. Getting to the banks is work in itself. And then you have to make sandwiches and a flask of coffee or soup, and hope that the evening before you had remembered that the tide would be floating the dinghy to get you out to the boat. You make sail, and if the wind is favourable, it's easy. If it isn't, it can take you the best part of an hour.

Once on the banks, the oystermen shoot their dredges, as near to 9 am as they can make it. The dredges are not large, at 3 feet or so across. They are made of iron, wood, string and interlocking wire rings that form a sort of lasting undersea chain-mail. They haven't changed much over the years, although by custom they are tailor-made for each man. Through the fishing day the oystermen trawl them over the banks, pulling them in when they think they have a fair catch, separating out on their 'cultch boards' all the rubbish and broken bottles that they pick up from the sea bed. Then, with their 'cull-tacks', a chisel-like tool, they prise off the stones that fix themselves to oyster shells. To help them keep to the bank as they dredge, the fishermen use landmarks – perhaps two houses in line, or a tree in line with a house, or two trees in line – which are known to no one except the crew of the boat.

This is the oyster fisherman's day: trawling the banks from end to end, under the most gentle of sail, and then turning, under the fastest sail they can raise, to start the run all over again. It is a day that theoretically ends at three in the afternoon but, like the oyster fisherman's mornings, the afternoons and evenings can get swallowed up by work. There is the beat back (although the boat's engine can be used for this, it still takes time), and there's always something to do to get ready for tomorrow.

Today, however, there are barely more than half a dozen oyster dredgers working out on the banks, whereas five years ago there were thirty, and a hundred or more half a century ago. The oystermen find a sort of bizarre consolation in the fact that today's pleasure-sailors are so keen on the gaff rig, which has served them well down so many years, and are buying up some of the old boats. Even so, few of them regard this trend entirely with approval. They look out of their River Fal cottages, over a stretch of river that has been, for most of them, their life, and wonder where it has all gone.

On the one hand, they are delighted that the superb design of their boats is being splendidly preserved, but on the other, one or two of them are enormously sad. As one former oysterman put it to me, 'What you get now are chrome winches and top sails, all the stuff that amateur seamen love. But these boats weren't built for that. They are *working* boats, and if they're not that, they aren't true.' As I looked from his window, I saw one of the few remaining oyster boats making its run. I had seldom seen a more delightful sailing sight. The boat took all the sail she carried as her hull muscled the tide. Then, as I watched, she turned and, with some sails lowered, became as gentle as could be.

One thing is certain. Few boats have ever been built which so superbly joined the wishes of builder and user, making it all the more ironic that these marvellous boats could, in the end, outlast the industry that gave them birth.

2
TRAINING UNDER SAIL
John H. Hamilton

What does a future officer in the West German Navy have in common with a young man keen on the navy who joins the British Sea Cadet Corps, and with a youngster not particularly interested in the sea who is seeking adventure: The answer is sail training.

The three sailing ships *Gorch Fock II, Royalist* and *Asgard II,* on which the young people mentioned might be found, have very different roles but also a great deal in common. Until the age of steam meant sailing ships were considered too slow, too unhandy and their schedules too unreliable, nearly all of them carried commercial cargoes; and without the deep-sea clippers, the coastal schooners and many other types of sailing craft, commerce would have been extremely restricted. Some of today's sailing vessels also carry cargoes – but they are human ones, consisting of young people engaged in different kinds of training.

The purpose of the great windjammer *Gorch Fock*, pride of the West German Navy, is to train future officers and petty officers in basic seamanship before they go on to the far more technical training required before they can take their places in the crews of modern warships filled with electronic equipment of amazing complexity. *Royalist* has a somewhat similar task; she was built specifically for the British Sea Cadet Corps and was designed for the express function of giving Sea Cadets (both boys and girls) the chance to get to sea and put into practice many of the seamanship skills that they have learnt in theory in their 'training ships' onshore. *Asgard* is in many ways similar to *Royalist* in appearance; however, her role is slightly different in that the young men and women from Ireland who sail in her are not particularly orientated towards the sea. They are from all walks of life – some still at school, some undergoing apprentice training, some sadly without jobs – and have been sent to take part in an adventurous voyage. They may never take to the sea again, but almost certainly they will have benefitted greatly from their time afloat.

Since the turn of the century the German nation has operated training ships for young men who would later become the officers and petty officers in their merchant and fighting navies. These include many famous names such as the original *Gorch Fock, Horst Wessel* and *Albert Leo Schlageter*, which have survived and are spoken of with pride wherever sailors get together. Prior to 1939 Germany had several such ships, but after the Second World War the *Pamir* and *Passat* were the only large sailing vessels in commission to train young seamen in addition to carrying cargoes.

Below: The German Navy ship *Gorch Fock*, with over 20,000 square feet of sail

However, in 1957 tragedy struck. The *Pamir* foundered off the Azores with the loss of eighty-six hands, with only six survivors. The disaster rocked not just West Germany but the whole world, and inevitably careful consideration had to be given to whether this kind of training for young people should be allowed to go on. Fortunately common sense prevailed and sailing ships, both large and small, continued in commission with their training tasks.

Two years before the *Pamir* disaster, the German Navy had decided to build a new windjammer to continue the work their ships had started before the War. A new *Gorch Fock* was actually in construction in the famous yard of Blohm & Voss at Hamburg, to a design similar to that of four existing training ships: *Eagle* in the USA, *Mircea* in Romania, *Sagres II* in Portugal and *Tovarisch* in the USSR. All work stopped because of the *Pamir* tragedy, but it was eventually restarted and the new ship was launched in 1958.

The *Gorch Fock* is a magnificent vessel with an overall length, not including the bowsprit, of 266 feet, a beam (width) of 39 feet, and she draws 16 feet. She is rigged as a three-masted barque, which is to say that she has squaresails on her two front masts (fore and main) but fore-and-aft sails on her mizzenmast. Squaresails are set on yards, long horizontal spares set at right-angles to the mast; all the others are fore-and-aft sails, including the four headsails or jibs, the staysails between the masts and the spankers behind the mizzenmast. She has twenty-three sails in all, giving a sail area of 21,011 square feet – nearly half an acre! The squaresails have marvellously salty names – course, lower and upper topsails, topgallants and royals – and tending them is a most challenging task for the young crews.

In addition to this enormous sail power, *Gorch Fock* has an auxiliary diesel engine of 1100 hp which can give her 10 knots through the water in calm conditions; none of these large sailing ships can motor at any reasonable speed when trying to force their huge masts, spars and rigging directly into a strong breeze. *Gorch Fock* takes her name from the famous German poet Johann Kinau, who wrote of the sea under the pseudonym Gorch Fock (*fock* being the German word for a headsail).

Before a squaresail can be set, a number of the crew, known as yardsmen, have to race aloft, using the rungs (or ratlines) as a kind of stepladder to get up to the yards; on *Gorch Fock* these are made of rope, but in *Royalist* and *Asgard* they are of wood. Then the yardsmen have to step out on to the foot-ropes and work their way out along the yard to their station. Once there, on orders from the mates on deck, they have to throw off the ropes (gaskets) that have been keeping the sail neatly stowed on the yards, thus allowing the sails to flop part of the way down, although they are still held in their gear, as it is called. This gear consists of the various controlling ropes, again with splendidly nautical names such as clewlines, buntlines and sheets.

Once the canvas has flopped down and when the captain is ready for the squaresails to be set, crew members on deck heave away on the sheets and slack off on the other ropes. Up aloft the yardsmen make sure that everything runs free, for should there be a snag it would hold up the operation of setting the sail. Some of the squaresails are set on yards which are not fixed to the mast but can be raised or lowered: these are the upper topsails, topgallants and royals. In the case of the *Gorch Fock*, those on deck have a Herculean task to raise the great yards, which with their sail and attendant ropes can weigh well over a ton each.

The cadets space themselves along the ropes which raise the yards (the halliards, or haul yards as they were originally called) and, on the command of their officer, race along the deck with the rope until they reach the side of the ship. Then the one furthest away from the mast races back and seizes hold again and so on, so that there is a continuous chain of heaving, running people in an elongated circle on deck. Above them, the great yards sway ponderously upwards with the heaving, flogging canvas slowly developing into the graceful curve that the sail assumes when set. Throughout these manoeuvres, the petty officers are controlling the work by the twittering of their bosun's calls, a sound which the cadets can hear above the roar of the wind, the hissing of the sea and the flogging of the half-set canvas.

Before they can descend to the deck the yardsmen have one final task, which is to overhaul (take the weight off) the buntlines (the ropes which will control the sail when it is time to furl it) by holding them up with a form of marine twine. If they do not do this, the weight of the buntlines themselves will pull at the sail and spoil its shape.

While the great squaresails are being set, other crew members are hauling on the foresail and staysail halliards and the spanker outhauls, and tending their other ropes. In a remarkably short space of time, perhaps less than ten minutes, up to twenty-three sails will have been set. The ship is turned from a rather gawky and unwieldly coot into a beautiful curvaceous swan, but something like 120 ropes will have been hauled or slacked and the main deck will, for a very short while, look like a spaghetti factory. This is dangerous because, if left, ropes can tangle themselves round each other, making it impossible to control the

Above: Yardsmen working in the rigging of the *Gorch Fock*

sails properly. An orgy of coiling now has to take place, and soon every rope is neatly stowed in its belaying pin, ready for trimming or whatever might need to be done next.

None of the above activities could ever be safely and efficiently carried out unless all 200 or so officers and crew worked as a team. From the captain on the quarter-deck, watching over the safety and heading of his ship, through the mates at the foot of the masts overseeing safety and action, to the cadets toiling, heaving and sweating to set the huge sails – even the cooks down below, making sure that all this energy will eventually be replaced by nourishing food – all are combining to get the ship under sail quickly, efficiently and safely. It is a splendid form of training; and if any crew member fails to pull his weight (so many everyday expressions acquire a vivid meaning on board sailing ships, whence they originated), extra work will fall on his watch-mates. It is also very apparent that all the tasks undertaken have a very real purpose: there is little need for the kind of petty or false chores to which some training schemes must resort. Here it is obvious that, if the ship is to get under way and be safely conducted over the ocean, anyone given a job has to do it to the best of his ability or the sea will find him out.

Throughout the time that the training ship is at sea, a large number of routine tasks have to be carried out. Steering – three great spoked wheels in the case of *Gorch Fock* – must be constantly attended, and the course ordered by the officer of the watch has to be maintained despite the vagaries of wind and wave. A careful lookout must be kept, for the ship is not all that handy and gone are the days when under all circumstances steam gave way to sail. Sometimes a 'steam-powered' ship is just as difficult to manoeuvre as a sailing ship and nowadays it frequently has a far deeper draft, which may greatly restrict where it can go. The navigators must ensure that at all times they know where the ship is and where it has to go next. In addition, a modern sailing ship cannot function without a multitude of electrical and electronic devices, all of which have to be operated and maintained, which means that generators have to be run to provide power.

With literally miles of rope and cordage, a constant eye has to be kept on the state of the standing and running rigging and a constant programme of maintenance and replacement takes place. Chafe, the action of one rope rubbing against another or against a part of the ship, must constantly be guarded against. It would be unfortunate, to say the least, if a rope rung or a foot-rope became chafed and thus lost its strength.

Meals have to be prepared and served – and washed up! Radio weather forecasts, vital to the ship's safety, must be monitored; paint has to be kept pristine; boats have to be maintained. There are 1001 things to be done, all essential, as the ship plies her way to her next port of call. *Gorch Fock* is, of course, also a school ship, and instruction is given for up to six hours a day in classrooms on board. Another speciality of this ship is the singing of sea shanties, in German, French, Spanish and English – often on deck during the commander's rounds.

Then there are various manoeuvres to be carried out. If a motor vessel wishes to change direction, she can usually do so by a turn of her wheel. Not so a sailing ship, because the relative direction of the wind to the ship determines whether she is running before it, has it on her beam (side) or is trying to make her way towards the direction from which it is blowing (known as 'beating into the wind'). This last manoeuvre is an uncomfortable and frustrating experience for a barque or any other type of square-rigger. A modern ocean-racing yacht can sail within about 30° from the direction of the wind, making her way to windward by a series of dog-legs or tacks until she eventually reaches her destination – or until the wind direction changes and allows her to sail to where she really wants to go. The square-rigger cannot do this; she can sail only within about 65° of the wind, so her dog-legs are through an angle of about 160°. It can therefore take a long time for her to reach a destination lying upwind.

As an example, the Danish sailing ship *Danmark* was once making her way south from the English Channel to Lisbon and the wind was firmly from the south. There was also an awkward and lumpy sea in the Bay of Biscay. The ship had managed to make her way to a position off Cape Finisterre when she took a long tack of 100 miles out in a south-westerly direction, then tacked and came back towards the coast. Yet, after covering 200 miles, she was back off Cape Finisterre, having made very little distance to the south!

These dog-legs or tacks are just one of several types of manoeuvres which big square-riggers have to make and once again they all require a great deal of teamwork and co-ordination of effort from the crew. In the case of a modern yacht, rigged with perhaps just two sails, one man on his own could probably manage tacking without too much difficulty by steering and working the jibsheets himself, while still keeping an eye out for other vessels. It would need some careful forethought but would by no means be impossible, and in yachts of 30 to 40 feet in length it is very often done.

The *Gorch Fock* is a different kettle of fish, however. Let's say the captain, sailing master or officer of the watch decides to tack. If conditions are anything but very light, it is probable that the watch on deck will not be sufficient in number to carry out the evolution, and either the stand-by watch or some of the day-workers – men employed in assisting the bosun, cook or others of the permanent crew – will have to give a hand.

In a small yacht with only two sails to be considered, one of those would look after itself because it is on a boom which 'self-tacks'; in the barque there may be as many as twenty-three sails set and of these only three do not need attention. So there would be the four jibs, each with a sheet to be let go at the correct moment – not too soon or the ship will lose way and fail to go through the eye of the wind, not too late or she will start to sail backwards! Then all the staysails between the masts are normally lowered.

What about the great squaresails? First of all, the courses – the large ones lowest down – have to be 'clewed up', then the yards have to be swung round so that their squaresails will be trimmed to the wind coming from its new apparent direction on the opposite side of the ship. This is achieved by letting go one set of braces and hauling on the other – easier said than done, because all this gear is very heavy and, although

Left: *Gorch Fock* crew
going aloft

the wind may help in some cases, it will hinder in others. Second, the swing must be at exactly the right moment in this manoeuvre, the yards on the mainmast being swung or braced first so that the squaresails continue to drive the ship forward as the wind comes from the other side. The sails on the foremast are left aback (with the wind blowing on their forward surfaces), which has the effect of helping to swing the bow of the ship through the wind. Once she is safely through and sailing on her new course, they and the headsails are trimmed for the new tack. The spankers at the aft (rear) end of the ship will have had their sheets tended so that they are positioned to help the manoeuvre.

In very light weather the minimum manning might be as few as forty-five; four helmsmen covering the three wheels, eight on the headsail or staysail sheets, fourteen to twenty on the yard braces, then perhaps ten standing by on the spanker plus some officers and petty officers to make sure everything is co-ordinated to the wishes of the officer of the watch. And, of course, someone must remember to tell the galley that the ship is going to tack: she will be heeling about 15° one way and then 15° the other, while the cooks are trying to prepare a meal for 230 people!

Tacking ship is just one of the manoeuvres that have to be performed. When the wind is coming from the back of the ship, say on the port (left) side, and it becomes necessary to bring it to the starboard (right) side, a wear-ship drill must take place, similar to what in a small yacht would be called a gybe. This time it is easier in the big ship, although there is still a great deal to do. Even a small alteration of course of, say, 30° means a great deal of sail adjustment when perhaps twenty-three sails have to be trimmed. Then comes the problem of too much wind. As the voyage continues, the wind may increase; or it may be getting near nightfall and the prudent captain may decide to furl his royals and topgallants – to snug the ship down for the night. A cry goes up: 'Stand by the sheets, clewlines and buntlines – yardsmen, lay aloft and stand by to stow the sails!' There is further scurrying around the deck, removing coils of rope from the belaying pins and throwing them in their coils on to the deck so that they will run without kinking. It seems chaos everywhere but is in truth a well-orchestrated manoeuvre.

The *Gorch Fock*'s crew at work is a joy to see. They are an efficient and well-drilled team and most can turn their hand to many tasks. It must be remembered that, as well as being a training ship in the Federal German Navy, she is also an ambassadress for her country; Germans are immensely proud of their square-rigger, which appears on the back of the 10-mark note as well as in a thousand pictures. Whenever she enters a port, every eye is upon her.

I remember seeing her take part in a 'Parade of Sail', with five other great windjammers, in the River Weser off Bremerhaven. She had to proceed up the river against the wind under engine and staysails, then round a buoy and set all her squaresails for just a couple of miles down the river with the wind behind her, before all sails had to be handed as she prepared to enter the lock and berth in the port. Just one hour after she had rounded the buoy, she had an awning rigged on her quarter-deck and a diplomatic party was in full swing. I was lucky enough to be one of the guests, and I could not resist asking one of the stewards serving drinks: 'What were you doing just one hour ago?

'I was aloft stowing the main royal,' he replied with pride and, I believe, some satisfaction, knowing that at least one of the guests realised that this ship was more than a rather unusual setting on which to hold a party.

Royalist is 97 feet long from her stern to the tip of her bowsprit, about a third the length of her German sister. She is therefore very much smaller but otherwise not so different. Her beam is 19½ feet, she draws ten feet, and she is rigged as a brig, which means that she has two masts, both of them carrying squaresails – like *Gorch Fock* without the third mast.

The Sea Cadet Corps operates a number of motor fishing vessels and launches as well as several small sail-training yachts to give its cadets some practical seagoing experience. In 1970 it was decided to build a larger flagship, so plans were laid for *Royalist*. She was designed, by the British naval architect Colin Mudie, very much on the lines of a small brig named HMS *Martin*, commanded by Admiral Lord Cunningham in 1901 and much praised by him as an ideal training vessel.

Royalist was built by the Isle of Wight boatyard of Groves and Guttridge and was named by Princess Anne in 1971. In her year of launch she won the Lloyd's Register Yacht Award for being the best-constructed, -designed and -equipped vessel for its purpose that year.

Royalist is a worthy flagship for the Sea Cadets and provides the opportunity for twenty-six young men and women to go to sea as trainees on each of her sail-training voyages. In the *Under Sail* television programme she was seen during one of the highlights of her year's training, taking part in the 1985 Cutty Sark Tall Ships' race from Chatham to Brugge, after which she sailed to Weymouth where she and most of the rest of the Sea Cadet Corps fleet of sailing and motor craft were reviewed by Prince Philip.

Royalist is manned by a small permanent crew consisting of the captain, sailing master, engineer, bosun, coxswain and cook. They are augmented by four other instructors who are on board for the same length of time as the cadets, usually periods of a week. These cadets are drawn from Sea Cadet units throughout the UK and, because they are from naval cadet units, the brig is run very much on naval lines.

As the description of *Gorch Fock*'s yards and squaresails shows, there is much work to do aloft in a square-rigger. It can be frightening at first, but gives a youngster an enormous sense of achievement. The brig rig is not good for going against the wind but is excellent when reaching or running before it, and as a training medium. When a modern sail-training yacht is coming into harbour, the relatively large crew does not have much to do; there will be a couple of cadets forward to tend the mooring lines and the same number aft, then another pair looking after the fenders; a rough stow will have been put on the sails and the remainder of the crew will not have a job so that, however keen they are, they will inevitably be standing around – often in the way. On a square-rigger, if the captain has timed things well, he will have ordered the squaresails to be clewed up, have sent his yardsmen aloft to put a harbour stow on the sails and will be using the remainder of the crew on deck to handle lines and fenders. If all goes according to plan, each group will have finished at about the same time and everyone will feel that he or she has done their bit towards getting the ship safely and neatly alongside. As a bonus, the lads aloft may well have impressed some of the local young ladies on the quayside – which will prove useful if shore leave is granted!

Like *Gorch Fock*, *Royalist* has auxiliary engine power, in the form of a pair of Perkins marine diesels of 115 hp each, which can push her along at a useful 6 knots unless she is trying to motor straight into the teeth of a blow.

Royalist is quite a photogenic ship. If you were to meet her at sea you might think, at first sight, that she was rather larger than she is. This is a

Below: *Royalist* **under sail in the 1985 Cutty Sark Tall Ships' race**

result of her design and her black hull with white 'gun-ports'. Perhaps a good indication of the success of her design is the fact that Colin Mudie, Morin Scott and other people involved in her design and operation were also asked to help with the design of the *Lord Nelson*, a barque built to give disabled people the chance of getting to sea as useful members of a crew, rather than as spectators who may be a liability.

Once signed on for a voyage in *Royalist*, the young man or woman will undergo an experience similar to that enjoyed by the naval cadets on board the German ship. Their voyage, usually of seven days, will probably take them from the port where they joined directly to a foreign port – say, from Gosport to Cherbourg – and thereafter where the wind dictates, for in a small square-rigger the well-known yacht hand's saying 'If I were a gennulman, Sir, which thank the Lord I'm not, Sir, I wouldn't never go to windward!' becomes particularly apt. The captain is encouraged by the shore organiser to plan his own route to make best use of the wind direction and other weather conditions. Steering, lookout, assisting with the navigation and in the galley, setting sails and trimming them in *Royalist* are all very similar jobs to those in her bigger sister, *Gorch Fock*.

One very important aspect of life on board is cleanliness. It is hard for anyone who has not experienced it to imagine thirty-six people living in the space available on board a sailing ship. Picture a rectangle 80 feet by 20 feet, then try to visualise within it thirty-six beds, two sitting or eating areas, a kitchen, refrigerators and larders, an engine room with fuel and fresh-water tanks, washbasins, lavatories – everything that the thirty-six people will need to live completely independent of the shore for at least a week. It can be done, of course, but under such circumstances cleanliness and neatness become essential – otherwise at best everyone will be living in a tangle of equipment and clothing, and at worst illness could spread throughout the crew.

Thus the daily cleaning hour, although a distinct shock for many of the youngsters, becomes a most important occasion, with the sailing master or the captain himself carrying out an inspection which would make the average mum sit up and take notice. Like so much of the training on board, this is done with a concealed discipline and a great sense of fun. It is quite common for whoever is inspecting to let fall the information that a deliberate 'plant' by the cadets will add spice to his rounds of the living spaces. This might be a coin or some other item hidden on a deck beam, or a written note underneath a lavatory seat. If he fails to find it, the cadets win a point; whereas if he discovers some genuinely grubby corner they have omitted to clean, he scores.

When they first arrive on board, the new crew members tend to think that all the ship's officers are ogres: the captain a remote figure living in a world of his own, the sailing master and coxswain living examples of Captain Bligh, Captain Morgan and Blind Pugh rolled into one. Perhaps they even glance around for a wooden leg and a parrot! Their original impressions are not changed, either, as with a roar they are rousted out on deck to tussle with a maze of unfamiliar ropes. However, as the voyage gets under way, a sneaking suspicion begins to emerge that perhaps there lurks a human heart within them after all, and by the end of the voyage they have learnt that the captain plays the guitar brilliantly and knows some great songs, the sailing master has a bark which would be the envy of any of his piratical forebears but has not bitten anyone throughout the voyage, and the bosun is always ready to show a new knot or exactly how to splice a Terylene rope. What is more, nearly every one of the young people will be hoping that somehow they will be able to return for another voyage.

It is very difficult to describe the effect on a young crew of a week in one of the smaller sail-training ships. In the case of *Gorch Fock*, the cadets are on board for some three months and this sea time is part of a general course – for the officer cadets, a term out of their curriculum at the Flensburg Naval Academy. Although the crew members of *Royalist*, come mostly from a uniformed cadet organisation, they will by no means all be going into the Royal or merchant navies. Of course, a proportion will, and it is probably for that reason that they joined the Sea Cadet Corps in the first place. The remainder, and they are a large proportion, will (perhaps without realising it) gain much more general benefits from their time on board ship.

It is not possible to teach the technicalities of the sea in so short a time; such skills as navigation, seamanship, boat-handling, rigging and ship maintenance all take considerable time and practice to absorb. As Geoff Ulrich, *Royalist*'s Captain, says, 'We're not going to make sailors out of them.' The young people will be learning self-discipline, self-reliance and the ability to work as one of a team and to live and function as a member of a close-knit community. All these qualities have a rather old-fashioned ring about them today, and may sound off-putting to some. In fact, such virtues are absorbed by those on board quite automatically and without anyone having to highlight them.

If a young man is given a job to do – for example, tying a rope on to the corner of a sail – he must tie it properly, tightly and with the correct

Above: Captain Geoff Ulrich and the *Royalist* officers

knot, otherwise it will either come undone while in use or – just as awkward – it will not come undone when it needs to be unfastened in a hurry. Failure may well be dramatic and will be seen by other members of his watch. It will be just as obvious to everyone if, when given some cleaning to do, he makes a poor job of it.

These are a series of tasks that are obviously not contrived, for each can be seen as important to the smooth running of the ship. Each must be done properly and the consequences of failure are obvious: this is good training, and it works. It is most interesting to observe a crew at the beginning and end of its time on board. At first you will see a bunch of silent individuals, nervously wondering what they have let themselves in for; at the end you will observe a laughing, happy team, half-delighted to be going home for a bath and some sleep and half-sad at leaving the ship and their newly made friends. They work hard, often harder than they imagined they were able, and they feel constantly tired because their sleep pattern is so different from what they are used to ashore, but it is enjoyable and worthwhile work and their prize is an efficiently sailed ship and a great sense of comradeship.

It is immensely difficult to express in words the character-building nature of sail-training, but those who form the permanent crews of the ships see it over and over again. It is their reward for extremely hard and dedicated work. The cadets' point of view is illustrated in the following extract from a letter one of them wrote to the chairman of the trustees who organise the sail-training scheme in which he took part:

> . . . A letter of complaint about your ferry service between England and Denmark. The ship leaked, rolled and pitched, was overcrowded and was very wet, I was cold, sick and damp and I thoroughly enjoyed myself. . . . The yacht performed with her usual high-strung femininity, leaking just the right amount to let us know how old she really is and the pumps gave up at the correct time to build up our characters. But she took the North Sea in her stride, she only got a few bruises, sorry we lost some of the sharp end but it looked very dramatic and impressed all the other boats. . . . There was a great international feeling among all the boats and we all made many foreign friends, especially among the Germans from the *Gorch Fock*. There was a strange brotherly feeling between us, despite the fact there were 200 of them and only 20 of us. The sea had brought about a bond between all the ships. . . .
>
> Most of the time in the rough weather I was wishing to be at home; now I am at home I am wishing to be at sea again.
>
> This is the first time I've written to a Lord, and I don't know how to end, so it's just
>
> Thank You!

Asgard, like *Gorch Fock*, is the second ship bearing her name. The first *Asgard* had an interesting career, starting off as a private yacht belonging to Erskine Childers, whose book *The Riddle of the Sands* is a yachtsman's classic. She was even involved in gun-running. Then she was owned by the Irish government and became their sail-training ship in 1968. She was very successful in her training role but eventually old age crept up on her and it was decided to put her on show in a dry dock at Kilmainham Jail, now a museum. She was temporarily replaced in her sail-training role by another yacht, the *Creidne*, until the present *Asgard* was ready.

A great deal of work went into the design of the new ship. The old *Asgard*'s captain, Eric Healy, and the designer, Jack Tyrell, had a good look round the existing small training ships so as to incorporate the best ideas from them all in their new vessel. *Asgard II* was named by the Irish Prime Minister in a great ceremony in 1981, after having been built at the Tyrell yard at Arklow. She is 104 feet long, with a beam of 21 feet and a draft of 9½ feet. She is rigged as a brigantine, which could perhaps be described as '*Gorch Fock* without her centre mast' – that is, with squaresails on the foremast but fore and afters on the main. Like nearly every sail-training ship she has a tight schedule to keep so needs auxiliary power, in this case a Kelvin 200 hp engine.

The trainees, both young men and women, who come to the *Asgard* are not future naval officers, nor are they members of a uniformed cadet organisation; they are just a mixture of young people. They may, for example, be from well-to-do homes, or they may be apprentices or

Below: The brigantine-rigged *Asgard II* under sail

junior firemen; they could be unemployed or perhaps even on pro-
bation. Between them they will represent a complete cross-section of
their country, which is precisely what the organisers want – for it is
largely this mixture which makes a success of the voyage for the crew.
Each one of them can see the strong and the weak points of their fellows,
can help where help is needed or, in turn, be helped. It is a curious fact
that the greater the differences between them, the greater the ultimate
effect the voyage seems to have.

One aspect of sail-training that often causes particular anxiety to the
trainee is going aloft. Indeed, this does not look too pleasant to the
novice, but no one is ever forced to do it. It is quite voluntary, although
very few fail to have a go and those who don't make it on their first
attempt will usually have conquered their fear before it is time to leave
the ship at the end of the voyage. More than that, once they have been
aloft for the first time it is often difficult to keep the young crew out of
the rigging!

'Sir, can I go aloft?' is a common request.

'You can when those five who are up there come down', might be the
reply. 'Oh, and don't forget to put on your safety harness. And report to
me when you're back down again.' (These are standard instructions
dictated by the safety requirements.)

When a new crew joins the *Asgard*, they are welcomed by Captain
Eric Healy and receive an initial briefing from the mate and the bosun.
Here are men with a great depth of knowledge, of the sea and of human
nature. Anyone who has served as permanent crew in a sail-training
ship knows – and ignores – the apprehension felt by even the toughest of
new crew members; they know that reassurance and patient instruction
has to be mixed with the firm establishment of discipline.

In all the training ships there is a rigid 'pecking order' on board – and
for a very good reason. It will seem strange, at first, that if the captain
wants something done, he will tell the chief officer (mate or sailing
master, as his deputy is variously known). The mate will decide which
watch should do the job and pass on the instruction to the watch officer
concerned, who will decide how many crew the job will need and in turn
brief his deputy who, ultimately, will decide which of the watch will
carry it out. Why couldn't the captain have briefed them direct? In
many cases, if he does there will be muddle because the captain, the
mate, the watch officer, the watch leader or even the bosun, the cook or
the coxswain could all give a poor wretched crew member jobs to do at
virtually the same time! The only way to achieve the teamwork needed

Above: *Asgard* **crew learning the value of teamwork**

to run the ship smoothly is to have this chain of command in which each leader knows the pattern.

The jobs of captain, mate and watch officer are probably obvious from their titles, but that of watch leader might need explanation. The crew is always divided up into two, three or occasionally four watches, which operate on a shift system so that everyone gets their fair balance of duty and sleep while the ship can continue safely for an unlimited time, both day and night. Each watch is commanded by a watch officer, who usually bears the complete responsibility for the conduct of the ship during the time his watch is on duty – that is, responsibility directly to the captain for the correct course being steered, avoiding of collision, ensuring that a safe amount of sail is set, maintaining of the ship's routine and so on. In addition, he is the boss of the members of his watch; he is assisted by a deputy who, in a large ship, will be a junior officer or a petty officer.

In a ship of the size of *Royalist* and *Asgard*, the post of watch leader provides an important opportunity for a youngster who has sailed on a previous occasion, has done well and has shown signs of having leadership ability to come on board again and act as a leader of the other young crew in his or her watch. This not only helps the young person concerned but also means that there is someone in the watch – living in the same conditions and close to the young crew – who can act as an example. Just by acting quite normally when the ship first gets to sea, when she heels over to the wind for the first time, when the sails flog a bit on being hoisted, the watch leader will help to establish confidence in the first-time voyager.

This watch leader has a most important role. Usually he or she is responsible to the watch officer for ensuring that each member of the watch is in the right place at the right time; that each has a fair share of steering the ship, acting as lookout, working in the galley, hauling on the heavy halliards or trimming the sheets of the lighter sails; and even that each gets his or her fair share of sleep.

Many of the young people fall in love with the sailing ships that they sail in and, thanks to the small number of jobs that there are for volunteer leaders, a few get the chance to sail again after their initial experience. Each ship has its own way of doing things, each has its own traditions. *Asgard* usually appears, when in company with other training ships, with a mascot not surprisingly named Seamus. Seamus will often be found safely tied to the fore-stay and correctly dressed in the rig of the day, sporting a safety harness and life-jacket.

I remember a time when I was fortunate enough to be invited to sail as a watch officer with Captain Eric Healy and was on watch as we sailed along the north coast of Spain. The wind, which was forecast to increase, was becoming a little too strong for the amount of sail we were carrying, so I nipped below to ask Eric if he wanted me to shorten sail.

'Have you asked Seamus?' he enquired.

'Er – no,' I confessed.

'Well, away and ask him, man,' ordered my captain.

What to do? Was he serious? What would the youngsters think if I was seen to go forward and have an earnest conversation with a doll? Or if I didn't! There is a nautical saying: 'Different ships, different long splices', so off I went, out on to the end of the bowsprit, where I had a short whispered consultation with Seamus. Then I returned to the captain.

'Seamus advises shortening sail, Captain.'

'Well, get on with it, then. What are you waiting for?'

The crew? They set to with a will to reef the main and hand two of the staysails. Of course, when in harbour with other training ships, Seamus leads a precarious existence, being much in demand as a prize of war.

And the brave ship that sports a Jolly Roger flag must be ready to defend her property at any hour of the day or night.

On another occasion I was doing a voyage in *Sir Winston Churchill*. We were secured in Cherbourg alongside our sister ship, *Malcolm Miller*. No Seamuses or Jolly Rogers were about, but I was surprised to see the mate of our sister ship on board, wearing his overalls. A sense of disquiet made me check round the ship, and when I opened the door of the captain's loo I was very surprised to see the complete apparatus missing. Just a flange was left, in the middle of the deck.

'Stop that man!' I roared at the watch keepers on the bridge. 'He's stolen the captain's loo!'

'He's drunk,' I heard them mutter.

'*I am not drunk*! Search the ship; I want him found.'

We ran him to ground in the bosun's half-deck store, in the process of hiding the apparatus in a dark corner. To cut a long story short, when we sailed an hour or so later, the other ship slowly hoisted a spare loo aloft in her mizzen rigging while our captain's binoculars tracked its progress. He was not amused, but the young crew were – highly. Of course, a ship must be run with a rigid routine and in a highly responsible manner. There is no room for sloppiness when dealing with the sea, but that does not mean there cannot be moments of fun as well.

One factor that is always born in mind in sailing ships of all sizes is safety. In every case there will be enough tried and tested people on board to serve the ship competently whatever conditions might come her way. They could reduce sail or get the ship to a place of safety even if every single one of the voyage crew of young people was overwhelmed by seasickness or fatigue. That is not to say that the young crew are not essential; they are. Without them the ship could not be sailed properly.

Safety is always in the forefront of the captain's mind and in the minds of his officers. Sailing is an adventurous activity and, like mountaineering, canoeing, horse-racing and other similar activities, it is probably the adventurous element that gives it an edge. It is curious that one first encourages the crew into a situation where there is an element of danger and then sets about minimising that danger with a set of rules and procedures. However, anyone engaged in these activities soon learns the benefits obtained by the participants and knows that, provided the rules are obeyed, the risk is minimal.

3
THE THAMES SPRITSAIL BARGE

Peter Ferguson

The Thames spritsail barge represents the final peak of development of a uniquely British and rather beautiful craft which evolved in the nineteenth century from the primitive sailing barges that frequented the London river up to the time of the Industrial Revolution. These vessels were little more than large open punts, flat-bottomed and with sloping ends, each carrying about 20–30 tons of cargo and setting a simple square sail on a pole mast. In time, as the size of the vessels increased, the fore-and-aft spritsail rig was more universally adopted.

This long-established rig, which had been familiar to the ancient Greeks and which in its European form is depicted in pictures and illuminated manuscripts from the fifteenth century onwards, derives its name from the massive diagonal spar which supports the large mainsail. This 'spreet', by which name it has been known to countless generations of bargemen, is of massive proportions. In today's barges it is usually made of hollow steel tube for cheapness, but traditionally it was fashioned out of a single length of Oregon or pitch pine averaging 55 to 60 feet from its heel to its joggle end with a girth of nearly 4 feet in the middle where the tapered spar is at its thickest.

The earliest accurate survey of a Thames barge can be traced to a remarkable book published in 1768 under the title *Architectura Navalis Mercatoria*. It contains an impressive collection of meticulously drawn plates depicting all kinds of craft from the largest line of battleship to the most humble working boat. The book was written by Frederick Chapman, who was at the time chief constructor of the Swedish navy. Among the drawings is one showing a small spritsail barge which Chapman describes as a chalk barge. The barge is 56 feet long and has a single pole mast with a sprit-rigged mainsail and large foresail. She also carries leeboards.

The Admiralty draughts deposited in the National Maritime Museum at Greenwich are another valuable collection of ship drawings which includes records of spritsail barges. Two sets of barge plans are preserved, the second of which, dated 1819, shows a 72-foot-long

Above: Thames spritsail barge *Edith* just after the Second World War

'swimmie' (the bargeman's term for a barge with 'swim' head and 'budget' stern, as the sloping box ends were described). The vessel, which was called *Ant*, had a beam of 20 feet 6 inches and a depth of 7 feet 4 inches, making her of comparable size to the later river staysail barges.

Steel's *Rigging and Seamanship*, published in 1794, gives an accurate description of the rigging of a late eighteenth-century Thames barge, and it is apparent from this account that barges of the period were just as likely to be rigged as a cutter or sloop as they were to be given a spritsail rig. However, by 1828, when E. W. Cooke's etchings of coastal sailing craft were published, the sailing barge was more finely developed. Cooke, who became a Royal Academician, left a legacy of beautifully drawn and accurately observed maritime studies, including many showing Thames barges. One lovely etching shows a large barge sailing off Northfleet on the Lower Thames. From her rig it is apparent that she was capable of undertaking long coastal voyages. She has a topmast and steeving bowsprit and a mizzen stepped on the massive rudder head. In addition to the full complement of fore and aft sails, she carries a square topsail and topgallant sail.

A few barges of similar description were still trading up to the First World War, albeit without square yards, but none had been built with swim head and budget stern since the mid-nineteenth century. This early hull form has, however, survived into our own time as the dumb lighter, which up to a few years ago could be seen by the hundred on the River Thames and in the dock systems all round the British Isles.

In 1902 Edward Lloyd Ltd of Sittingbourne, the Kent paper-making company, had one of these wooden lighters built locally at a cost of about £700, and named her *Montreal*. She spent her whole working life with Lloyd, whose successor Bowater sold her in the early 1970s to a young Medway shipwright, Owen Emerson. He converted *Montreal* to sail following the example of E. J. & W. Goldsmith Ltd, who had rigged the 78-ton lighter *Atom* as a spritsail barge over half a century earlier, before the First World War.

I well remember the first time I saw *Montreal*. I had travelled to Hoo for the Medway Race, arriving late the night before, and in the morning I awoke just as dawn was sending its pale gold and silver light across the Medway. There was no puff of wind anywhere to create even a single cat's paw over the water, and the river was a shimmering mirror image of the clear sky, the distant shoreline and the silhouettes of the eight or ten barges riding quietly to their anchors. It was then that I spotted *Montreal* – 'stumpy-rigged', for she had not yet received her topmast – with her swim head and budget stern, her profile an anachronism even as she lay surrounded by other barges. I felt as though I was looking at a delicately executed watercolour from a previous century.

Owen Emerson eventually sold *Montreal* and in December 1974 bought the Ipswich-built 'sprittie' *Victor*, which he rebuilt and rerigged in the space of eighteen months. *Montreal*, after a spell of inactivity laid up at St Katharine's Dock in London, was also rerigged, and over the past decade has taken part in the annual barge races, where despite her unusual appearance she has acquitted herself with dignity. Improvements to her rig have made her rather faster than one might imagine and, given favourable conditions, she has outsailed many of the slower conventional spritsail barges.

Opposite: *Constance* unloading at Milton Creek in Kent, about 1900

Another barge which started life with swim head and budget stern was the old *Favorite* (the spelling is correct). Built by John Huggens at Crown Quay, Sittingbourne, in 1803, she traded out of Milton Creek for over sixty years before being so damaged by collision that her stern had to be completely rebuilt. By this time the modern barge stern had been developed and the old barge was given the new look. As well as building barges, John Huggens opened one of the first brickworks in Sittingbourne, thus starting the industry which culminated in the vast Smeed Dean brick empire. London was expanding rapidly in the nineteenth century, and millions of the familiar yellow stock bricks were carried to the city by sailing barge.

After Huggens died in 1865, his son eventually disposed of his fleet of sailing barges, and in 1869 George Smeed acquired *Favorite* for £150. She continued to trade for the firm for a further seventy years before being sold in the mid-1930s for conversion to a yacht, having been in trade for an incredible 130 years.

Favorite very nearly didn't reach her century, however, for in 1898 she was run down by a steamer and lost her old swim head. She was salvaged, and during rebuilding at Sittingbourne was given a conventional barge bow. Thus her transformation was complete, although her midships section was still the original and continued so until her demise. This came in 1966 when the old vessel was quietly living out her days as a houseboat at Chiswick Eyot on the Thames, providing a comfortable home afloat for a retired air pilot, Gordon Wansbrough-White. When repair work had to be undertaken to the river bank where she was moored, *Favorite* was laid to temporary moorings in the tideway, and one weekend when her owner was away she mysteriously sank – struck by a passing ship during the night, some people thought. Being a threat to navigation, she was hastily removed by the river authorities with drag chains to a safer part of the river, but this was too much for the old barge and she became a constructive total loss.

The following weekend, to get away from it all, a sorrowful Gordon Wansbrough-White went sailing on the Thames Barge Sailing Club's *Asphodel*. I was also part of the crew on that occasion, and Gordon told me how he had managed to salvage only one of his collection of old 78-rpm records from the wreck. It was of Paul Robeson singing 'River Stay Away From My Door'!

By the 1860s, then, the barge was beginning to resemble the craft we know today. The promotion of barge racing at this time led in the years

46

that followed to finer points of refinement. Wheel steering began to supersede the enormous tillers during the 1870s, which in turn permitted the mizzen to be stepped inboard and no longer on the rudder head. The sail became larger but its function was still primarily to help the helmsman by pushing the stern around when the helm was put down, this being achieved by sheeting the sail to the rudder blade.

The old tillers could be as long as 18 feet and embellished with carved ornament, and I remember many years ago talking on the subject to Harold Farrington-House when he was Club Skipper to the Thames Barge Sailing Club. Sitting on the deck of *Asphodel*, anchored off the derelict pier at Sheerness – long since demolished – he began to tell me about Burley's barge yard near his home town of Sittingbourne, which had just recently ceased all commercial activity and was in danger of falling into ruin or worse. All the buildings were still there; the barge-building shed with blocks alongside, the two-storey sail loft and a small single-storey timber-framed forge. It represented one of the most complete small shipyards still left in the southeast of England.

However, it was the old forge that Harold particularly wished to describe to me, knowing my keen interest in barge history. He then went on to describe in detail the construction of the building, explaining that the roof was supported on huge tiller bars which had come out of sailing barges. Some two years later the Society for Spritsail Barge Research issued a prospectus for the restoration of Burley's yard to provide a working museum and amenity area on the banks of Milton Creek. The scheme gathered momentum and culminated in the formation of the Dolphin Yard Sailing Barge Museum which, despite past administrative problems, brings pleasure to many summer visitors.

An interesting throwback to the days of tiller steering may be seen in the little stumpy barge *Lady of the Lea*, which can claim to be the very last wooden spritsail barge ever built. Constructed by Hyam and Oliver at Rotherhithe for HM War Department Service at Waltham Abbey and Woolwich Arsenal as late as 1931, she was rerigged a few years ago by a young couple who had made their home on her. In her restoration they used plans which I reconstructed in 1975 from a faded photograph of the original Admiralty blueprint lent to me by Arthur Bennett, whose early books on barging, *June of Rochester* and *Tide Time*, have delighted many a sailing-barge enthusiast.

Lady of the Lea has been restored to her original tiller steering. This made her a suitable candidate for the BBC's dramatisation of *December Rose*, for the film is set in the era before wheel steering became the accepted norm. Filming took place during November 1985, with the Waterways Depot at Leeds transformed into nineteenth-century London dockland. The Maldon stack barge *Dawn* and the Humber sloop *Amy Howson* were also called in to take part.

Another location chosen was the Walton Backwaters in Essex, setting for the much-loved Arthur Ransom stories. The *Dawn* and *Lady of the Lea* were moored at Landermere Quay, which the late Bill Kennett from Sittingbourne visited in 1910 in the sailing barge *Mercy* when he was her mate. Skipper Kennett once said that the quay derived its name from smugglers who used to say, 'Land 'em 'ere!' True or false, the quay, which is reached by a narrow straight cut about a mile long, is a remote enough place, better known to some people as Beaumont Quay. The massive stones forming the quay wall were taken from the medieval London Bridge, built in 1176 and dismantled in the 1820s.

Below (left to right): Coasting barges *Marjorie*, *Millie* and *Saltcote Belle* in the Stour estuary near Harwich

Dawn has wheel steering, so before filming commenced she returned to the place where she had been built, Walter Cook's barge yard at Maldon, where shipwright Ian Danskin replaced her wheel gear with an 18-foot-long oak tiller.

When wheels began to be fitted to barges, the familiar ship's wheel, brass-bound and made of teak, became standard for the big coasting barges, as indeed it was for most coastal sailing ships of the late nineteenth century. A coasting barge was normally fitted with a steeving bowsprit and her hull was more massively built, with a pronounced sheer and finer run and entrance, to cope with sea-going conditions.

The river barge, in contrast, rarely ventured beyond the confines of the Thames estuary. Apart from her countless short trans-shipment voyages up and down the London river with every conceivable cargo, she was used mainly for transporting bricks and cement from the Medway through the Swatch Way and Sea Reach to London with 'rough stuff' back, or through Sea Reach and up Swin to the creeks and farms of Essex with the street sweepings from London's horse-drawn traffic, to return with a cargo of hay for the horses' bedding and fodder.

'Rough stuff' was the polite way of describing one of the most obnoxious of all cargoes carried, but also one of the most frequent. This was household refuse which, in the words of Skipper Harold Farrington-House, who often carried it to Sittingbourne, 'stank something rotten, but you got used to it'. This was probably an understatement, for I well remember many years ago sailing on the Thames down-wind of a tug towing half a dozen lighters piled high with the awful stuff. The seething mass was smouldering under the process of spontaneous combustion and the stench at even a hundred yards' distance was enough to snatch your breath away.

'Rough stuff' was used in the brick-making industry, for it contained a high proportion of cinders and ash in those smog-polluted days before smokeless fuels were introduced. The mixture of this ash with the clay before firing produced an extremely hard and durable brick, and this happy coincidence did much to solve one of nineteenth-century London's most difficult problems, that of dispersing the huge mounds of rubbish, immortalised by Dickens in *Our Mutual Friend*, which were scattered around the boundaries of inner London by the private contractors who collected it.

One such contractor, who amassed a considerable fortune and earned himself the title of 'Golden Dustman', was William Henry Dodd. When he died in 1881 he left nearly £100,000. Among many bequests to various charities was one of £5000 to the Fishmongers' Company to be invested, the interest so gained to be distributed in part to poor bargemen while the rest was to be used to provide prizes for the annual sailing match. Dodd had owned a sizeable fleet of sailing barges, and in 1863 he instituted the Thames Sailing Match to raise the status of the bargeman and encourage builders to improve the design of the spritsail barge. The venture was an unqualified success and achieved all that the 'Golden Dustman' had hoped. Barge builders, commissioned by owners anxious to win the coveted race trophies, turned out faster and sleeker barges often launched and entered for the race on the same day.

Barge races were not entirely new in 1863, for the first recorded race was held in 1844 at the Harwich Regatta, when three spritsail barges raced for a purse of £8. However, by the end of the nineteenth century, with the Thames and Medway races firmly established as national events, the pinnacle of barge design was reached in 1897 when James Piper of Greenwich built the champion of champions, the famous *Giralda*, especially to compete in the Diamond Jubilee Barge Match. She won the race four consecutive times between 1897 and 1900, and again in 1904, 1905 and 1908. She was also Medway champion four times, and during her racing career seldom finished without a place. In 1903, when she was beaten into second place by less than a minute, she sailed the 58-mile course in 5 hours 12 minutes 5 seconds, an average speed of over 10 knots. Above the waterline she looked flatter than many barges, but below she was a masterpiece. She had a pronounced rounded forefoot and a fine entry which merged effortlessly into the flat bottom. Her run was very long, starting amidships and ending well tucked up into her graceful transom stern. Her bottom was well rockered so that she drew considerably more water in the middle than at each end. Despite these refinements her stowage capacity was good and she had a useful working life of nearly fifty years.

River work upstream from the Pool of London and on the upper Medway meant passing under fixed bridges, and for this reason the Thames barge never stepped its main mast through the deck and on to the keelson. Instead, the mast was housed in a wooden (later steel) mast case bolted to the main deck between the wide fore and main hatches. This mast case was supported in turn on heavy wooden sailing beams and the weight transferred to the keelson by vertical fixed posts in the ship's hold.

This arrangement enabled the mast and all the gear to be lowered to deck (the topmast first having been lowered), the weight being taken by the massive 4-inch steel-braided forestay looped around the top of the mainmast, and led to the stay fall tackle shackled to an iron ring in the top of the stem band. The stay fall tackle consists of two triple-sheaved iron blocks and a fall of 2¼-inch galvanised wire 25 fathoms long. When lowering the gear, this fall is led to the windlass barrel and roved round for several turns, being carefully surged round while the gear is lowered. The enormous purchase power of the triple blocks enables the work to be accomplished fairly easily by two men.

When 'shooting' bridges, the skipper would generally pick up a third hand at some convenient spot below the bridge to help the barge crew with the complicated manoeuvre to follow. The 'huffler', as he was known, was often himself a retired barge skipper and also a man with local knowledge of every set of tide and trick of wind around the bridges. It was all a matter of split-second timing: the barge sailed on course to take it through the required arch of the bridge, and at the precise moment the gear would be lowered away sufficiently to clear the bridge, losing as little way as possible.

The momentum achieved had to be sufficient to clear the bridge before the crew could heave up the gear again. Since the sails were left set when the gear was lowered, they quickly filled away and the vessel proceeded on her journey, having dropped the 'huffler' who returned below bridge to pick up his next charge. However, it wasn't always as simple in practice as in theory. The late Vic Wadhams, who had passed under Rochester Bridge countless times in his long sea career in sailing barges, told me that it sometimes took several attempts at the operation before a barge was safely through.

On the journey up from the Pool of London there are twenty-six fixed bridges across the Thames between London Bridge and Teddington Lock, and for this reason many barges making the journey up or down the length of the tidal river would leave the gear lowered and rely instead on a 'bridge sail'. The mizzen was always left standing, as its height did not restrict the barge's passage under the bridge arches. The crew would therefore rig a short temporary pole mast forward, on which was set a light square sail on a yard, and by working tides this gave sufficient steerage way to accomplish the journey.

When the gear is lowered, the sprit is allowed to settle on deck – always to starboard of the wheel and mizzen – while the mainmast and lowered topmast rest on a wooden prop standing on deck just forward of the main horse. The truck of the topmast and the barge bob (owner's flag) are therefore directly above the wheel, which as a result is vulnerable to damage if the gear is lowered too far or too heavily. Big cast-iron wheels were therefore preferred for river barges because they were less likely than wooden ones to be smashed in an accident. Their distinctive swirl pattern earned them the name 'chaff cutters' because, apart from the eight wooden spokes fitted into the rim, they resembled the cast-iron wheels used for much of the heavy farm machinery of the period. These wheels were not as a rule found on any other type of sailing craft.

I have restored one of these 'chaff cutters', and it makes a most unusual ornament in my house. It is very heavy, as much as one man can lift. I bought it years ago, via an intermediary, from the owner of the 'sprittie' *Persevere*, who no longer wanted it because the barge had become a static houseboat at Conyer Creek off the Swale, in Kent. The barge was moored close by the famous barge yard of Alfred Marconi White where, between the years 1890 and 1914, forty-four sailing barges were built, including some of the most successful racing barges of all time, such as the beautiful *Sara* of 1903.

Persevere's master in trade for over twenty years had been Fred Cooper of Great Wakering in Essex, who, finding life on motor barges too frustrating after the last war, went back to his old love of sail by rerigging and skippering yacht barges. By the 1950s these were beginning to re-emerge and gradually supersede the dwindling fleet of trading barges. Fred was a painstaking maritime historian and published two books on barges which have become standard reference works. He also gave freely of his time and talents to anyone with an interest in his beloved spritsail barges and, until his untimely death a few years ago, was of inestimable help to me in my early years as editor of *Topsail*. The standard of accuracy which that magazine has achieved is due in no small measure to Fred's influence.

When I first acquired *Persevere*'s wheel, I excitedly telephoned Fred to tell him the news. He began to reminisce about his days on the old barge, telling me that mine was at least the third wheel to be installed in the barge in his memory. The first two, he told me, had been wooden wheels, and both were smashed in the dock work and in raising and lowering the gear.

Throughout the long period of the barge's development, the flat bottom and slab sides of the hull design remained unchanged. They merged in a sharp angular chine that ran the length of the vessel's midship section and was cleverly worked into the short run and entrance, producing a hull that was cheap to construct and maximised cargo space. In constructing a barge the keel, a plank of elm wood 12 inches wide and 4 inches thick, was laid, and floors of 8-inch-by-6-inch English oak crossed after setting up the massive oak stem and stern posts and their associated deadwood at each end of the keel.

Over the floors and immediately above the keel was laid the huge keelson, which was usually a baulk of Oregon pine up to 18 inches square, running the whole length of the barge in one piece, being scarfed into the deadwood behind the stem and stern posts. This was the barge's backbone which gave the vessel its great strength. The floors were half-jointed at the outer ends to receive the frames, which were in one straight piece except at each end which was curved and therefore of grown oak. Bottom and side chines of 16-inch-by-3-inch elm plank were used to cover the sharp angle thus produced, and these in turn were worked into the run and entrance at the ends of the hull. This differed from the normal practice for round-bilged vessels where the frames had to be made up of curved floors, futtocks and top timbers scarfed together in at least six pieces to the cross-section, compared with only three straight pieces used in the cross-section of a barge hull. For further strength, 12-inch-by-6-inch inner chines or side keelsons of pitch pine were fitted to the inside of the frames where they were jointed to the floors.

The other major difference in construction between the barge and her deep-water sisters was the use of tar-and-hair set work in place of the usual wooden ship-building practice of caulking the seams with oakum and pitch after the planking was fixed. As work proceeded on a barge's bottom planking, which was usually in 3-inch Oregon pine, it was rabbetted and the joints filled with tar and elk or cow hair. The planks were drawn together by chains and a bottle screw before being bolted through the floor timbers and ceiling, and this tightening-up operation gave a good waterproof job. The barge's side planking was usually of two 1½-inch skins of pitch pine or oak similarly rabbetted and set with tar and hair. Inside the frames a pine lining 2 inches thick was used, and the barge hull thus became a double-skinned box, immensely strong and, because of the set work, flexible when taking the ground and drying out between tides, which was an essential feature of a barge's working life.

The flat bottom produced a vessel that was extremely shallow for her size and stowage capacity, and the barge was therefore able to sail over water denied to her deeper-keeled counterparts around the coast. This was especially suited to the Thames estuary and the east coast, which harbours some of the most dangerous shoal water to be found on any coast. Not only that, but a great many of the destinations reached by the barges were little more than shallow ditches covered only at high water, and the barge's ability to be 'poked' up these creeks to the farms and mills of East Anglia and to the mud holes in the River Medway to load brick-making clay, for example, was at the very heart of their economic viability.

However, all this would have been impossible but for the ingenious device known as the leeboard. Leeboards are the massive 18-foot-long, fantail-shaped oak boards which are pivoted to each side of the barge by a toggle above the covering board at a point just behind the forward shroud. The boards are raised and lowered by means of hand winches aft, adjacent to the wheel. When sailing to windward, the leeboard on the weather side is lowered to act as a deep keel, like the centre board or drop keel of a racing dinghy. Without it, as every dinghy sailor knows, the vessel would sag very badly to leeward and its sailing efficiency over the water would be reduced dramatically. The leeboard is absolutely essential to the barge's progress when sailing light to windward, but in its trading days, when deep-loaded to the point where the deck amidships would be awash, a barge in a strong breeze and well heeled over could sail on the lee chine edge.

The purpose of the leeboard can baffle even intelligent onlookers. Skipper Horace Briggs told me a story illustrating this when he was master of the coasting barge *Ethel*, which crossed the Atlantic in 1978 on the deck of a steamer for use on the Great Lakes and the eastern seaboard of North America. In 1973 she was under charter to Gestetner, carrying a floating trade exhibition around the coasts of Great Britain. She had made the voyage west and into the Bristol Channel and was lying safely at Castle Quay, Barnstaple, in North Devon. Spritsail barges were never seen in large numbers in the Bristol Channel, although a few were owned there and others occasionally traded as far. The unusual sight of a large sailing vessel in the harbour drew crowds of onlookers to the quay, and Horace and his mate, from the sanctuary of the skipper's cabin, heard one 'knowledgeable' admirer explain in great detail to his assembled audience how the leeboards were flapped up and down in the water to propel the barge along!

Ethel was built in 1894 at Harwich by the Cann brothers, John and Herbert, builders of great repute who, between the years 1877 and 1914, turned out twenty-seven sturdily built sailing barges, eleven of which are still afloat today. Their longevity and endurance owed much to the quality of their construction, but it also had a lot to do with the fact that many of these surviving Harwich coasters were built for local owners and engaged for most of their working lives in the Ipswich-to-London grain trade. They had therefore to be kept completely watertight, or damage would occur to their vulnerable cargoes with devastating results.

Ethel was originally owned by the Holmes family of Harwich before being sold to W. Ellis of Ipswich, but in 1928 she was bought by Cranfield Brothers Ltd, the Ipswich millers. She was unrigged in 1955 and fitted with a diesel engine, continuing to trade until 1971 when she was sold to Tate and Lyle Group Services Ltd, who were already operating the *May*, another Cann-built grain barge. Before being shipped over to America, *Ethel* completed a circumnavigation of England, Wales and Scotland via the Caledonian Canal in 1974 and 1975.

Left: *May*, one of eleven grain barges built by John and Herbert Cann at Harwich which are still sailing today

55

One of *Ethel*'s sister ships, built by the Cann brothers in 1901 and of the same registered tonnage, is the *Gladys*, featured in the BBC television series *Under Sail*. *Gladys* measures 84 feet in length, with a beam of 20 feet 6 inches. Her registered tonnage is 68, giving her a cargo capacity of about 140 tons. She was originally owned, until 1912, by William Thomas Whitmore of Harwich and then sold to Cranfield Brothers and employed in the grain trade alongside the barges *May, Kimberley, Ethel, Spinaway C* and *Orinoco*. She was still trading under sail alone after the Second World War, becoming an auxiliary in 1950 before being finally reduced to a motor barge six years later. Cranfield Brothers sold their remaining fleet of ex-sailing barges during the late 1960s and early 1970s, and in 1973 *Gladys* was purchased by Weston Shipping, now Mardorf Peach and Co. Ltd, and taken to Maldon, Essex, where she was rerigged at Cook's barge yard the following year. Since 1975 she has been a regular contestant in the annual barge matches, with an impressive record of successes. For much of that time she has been sailed by Dick Cresswell, her skipper for the match featured in the *Under Sail* programme.

It is with sadness that I have to record Dick's passing early in 1984. He had been 'in the barges' for close on fifty-eight years, all his working life except for a brief spell on a farm as a boy. Born and brought up in East Anglia, Dick Cresswell left school when he was twelve and by all accounts was not considered to be particularly academic, for his schoolmaster challenged him to find a job if he was capable of it! So Dick went barging and became mate on an old 38-ton 'sprittie' called *Arthur & Eliza*, which had been launched at Faversham, Kent, way back in 1862, and was then managed by John Sparrow of the Bristol Arms Inn, Shotley, Suffolk. His skipper was Bill Salt, whom Dick remembered as being 'a very fast chap who took about a month to do a freight'! What Bill Salt lacked in speed, he made up for in sound advice, and the young Dick Cresswell soon found himself a mate's job on Fred Horlock's *Reliance*, a much newer barge specially built for the Horlocks at Ipswich by W. H. Orvis in 1900.

The skipper of *Reliance* was Captain 'Dod' Newman, who fourteen years earlier in 1912 had taken as his first command the sailing barge *Valentine*, owned by the Essex millers W. Green & Sons of Brantham. After three years 'Dod' transferred to the *Orion* which, much later, became famous as the *Gold Belt*, a star of the BBC's wartime radio broadcasts under her owner-master John Corello, who had the unusual distinction of a double career as a barge master and successful operatic tenor on the London stage.

Above: *May* **(left) and** *Gladys* **racing from Pin Mill**

'Dod' Newman relinquished command of the *Orion* in 1918, when he joined Fred Horlock of Mistley and took that company's barge *D'Arcy* for three years. He then transferred to Horlock's *Edme*, another Cann-built barge like the *Gladys*, before taking the *Reliance* in 1924. When Dick Cresswell joined him as mate in 1926, it was the start of a partnership that was to last for some years. In 1929 Horlock was building at Mistley the steel 'sprittie' *Adieu*, named after one of the company's racehorses, and 'Dod' Newman was appointed her first master. When she was launched he had the job of fitting her out from a bare hull, and on 3 December that year set sail on her maiden trip with Dick Cresswell as mate to load acid at Silvertown on the Thames for the B.X. factory at Brantham. After adjustments to her rig, she proved to be one of the fastest barges sailing out of Mistley.

They loaded an assortment of dry cargoes, the most regular being malt, barley, sugar, oil cake and other animal feedstuffs, pollards and bran, and traded between Mistley, London, Ipswich, Woodbridge and Colchester, with an occasional trip to Great Yarmouth. Dick Cresswell remembered with clarity these cargoes, for in many places the skipper and mate loaded the barges themselves – back-breaking

Above: Fred Horlock's *Reliance* (right) at Mistley in the 1930s

work humping heavy sacks – for which they received no extra wages. There were anomalies: malt they loaded themselves, but flour was always handled by the dockers. When he started with Horlock, Dick considered it a good week if he earned 50 shillings (£2.50). The best cargo, he reckoned, was bran at 7s 6d (37½p) per ton, and the worst was oil cake, his mate's share of a 100-ton cargo being £3 12s 9d (£3.63).

Payment was by the traditional method of 'shares', so that if a freight was worth, say, £40, and dock dues and other disbursements had reduced the sum to £30, the owner of the barge would take half and the skipper and mate divided the remainder two thirds to one third, so that shares in this case would be £15, £10 and £5. There was usually a guinea gratuity paid on delivery, which theoretically should have been shared, but by custom had become the skipper's jealously guarded 'perk'. Such was the case under 'Dod' Newman, and Dick Cresswell recalled that, shortly before he left Horlock for a brief spell in the big Everard steel coaster *Greenhithe* under skipper Frank Ellis, he had been called into the office at Mistley to see Fred Horlock concerning the customary gratuity. The boss, mindful of the fact that he was losing 10s 6d (52½p) per freight, and not liking to confront his skipper direct, thought he might find an ally in the young mate, whose share would have been worth 3s 6d (17½p). Dick Cresswell's answer was unexpected: 'One day Fred Horlock said to me, "You'd better come in the office, Mr Mate." I says, "What for?" He says, "This guinea gratuity, if that went on the freight you'd have a little bit of it, so, young man, what are you going to do about it?" So I says, "Well, I reckon about going skipper one day and I want that guinea!" Everyone thought I would give in to the old man, but I didn't, you see!'

Within eighteen months Dick Cresswell had been promoted skipper, and the guinea gratuity stayed with the skipper in time-honoured custom!

In the last few years we have witnessed the passing of the older generation of barge skippers who, born at the turn of the century, grew up at a time when some 2000 barges were registered and trading. But that golden heyday, which had reached its peak between 1880 and 1910, was already over when Dick Cresswell's generation was born. At the end of the First World War the number of barges registered had dropped to 1650. Wartime neglect, a shift in the balance of traditional trades and the mounting competition from foreign steam and motor coasters were beginning to take effect.

The appalling economic depression of the 1920s and 1930s saw the dwindling barge fleet reduced to a mere 600 by the time war was declared again in 1939. Tier upon tier of laid-up barges were to be seen in the Thames and elsewhere, their sails and hulls rotting through enforced idleness and neglect. The infamous moorings at Woolwich became known as the 'starvation buoys'. Barges which had been built thirty or forty years previously for about £1200 could be bought for as little as £200. Yet, in spite of this decline, a few owners were still building new barges right up to 1930, most notably the Horlock family at Mistley in Essex, who built a number of fast steel sailing barges for their own use. Most of these later 'ironpots' are still sailing today, having been rerigged following post-war conversion into motor barges.

With the onset of the Second World War, many barges were commandeered for Ministry of War Transport service as mine watchers, storage hulks for ammunition and powder, barrage-balloon platforms, and a host of other static duties. Their sailing gear was removed and thus they remained for the duration of hostilities, gradually being weighed down below the waterline by marine growth and subjected to fatal attacks by wood-boring worm. By the end of the War few were fit for further service. However, some of the fleet fared better and continued to trade the now perilous sea lanes, helping to keep essential supplies on the move. The crews had to face the constant threat of magnetic mines and enemy aircraft attack, and were subjected to Admiralty restrictions which forbade movement by night.

To skippers used to working tides, the nine-to-five philosophy of the Naval patrols was very frustrating, as it could prove disastrous in foul weather to have to put the hook down and anchor off some lee shore just

Below: Barges laid up at Greenwich before the Second World War

because it was sunset and the Navy had decreed it. No wonder, then, that many skippers found ways to dodge the system. Dick Cresswell, who was skippering Horlock's steel barges at the time, reckoned he led a charmed life during the War. His barges were all fast and in good condition and he was regularly running freights from London to Ipswich, Mistley and Great Yarmouth.

On one occasion, bound from London, he was sailing over the Spitway and into the Wallet opposite Clacton when sunset forced him to obey the Admiralty rule. Dick stowed the sails and lowered the anchor, but held it just off the bottom, thus continuing to drive down with the tide. After a while a Naval patrol boat approached him and reported that his anchor appeared to be dragging, as the barge was now 5 miles further up the coast than when he had last been sighted. Tongue in cheek, Dick told the young naval officer that his anchor must be made of wood and therefore floating, and he made a pretence of letting go a bit more anchor chain, but not enough to hold the barge. That night they crept down past Walton Backwaters and saved themselves some passage time right under the nose of the Royal Navy.

Another trick they adopted was that of wrapping bits of old rag around the windlass gear to deaden the familiar 'clank, clank, clank' of the engaging pawl as the anchor was lifted. That way, nobody heard them get under way in the dead of the night to steal a few precious hours of tide when they should have been riding to their anchors until daybreak. Dick's brother, who was mate with him, used to get very worried about being caught once too often by the authorities and hauled up in court, but they were never apprehended and Dick explained that as they sailed for turn – that is, the first barge in port got the return cargo – the risk was financially essential to their livelihood.

A number of sailing barges took part in the evacuation of the British Expeditionary Force from the Dunkirk beaches in 1940. At least sixteen went across and some, like the huge steel-built barges *Ethel Everard, Aidie* and *Barbara Jean*, were abandoned on the beaches, never to return. Only seven barges got back, all under heroic conditions, bringing with them survivors from that terrible ordeal. Among those still sailing today are R. & W. Paul's company barge *Ena* and the Thames Barge Sailing Club's charter barge *Pudge*, which carries a bronze plaque in her saloon commemorating her role as a 'Dunkirk Little Ship'.

Other groups of barges were requisitioned for war service in the Bristol Channel and in Scotland, where no less than twelve made their home in the unfamiliar waters of the Clyde estuary. Most were stripped of their sailing gear, which was stored ashore, and relied on motors for the duration of hostilities. The barges were used for ferrying duties in and around the estuary and as far as the Outer Hebrides. Several of these are still sailing as yacht barges, among them the *Scone*. Her skipper at the time, the late Harry Bagshaw, recalled that one job they had undertaken was to ferry Winston Churchill across the Firth of Clyde to a waiting cruiser when he made his historic wartime journey to the United States. It was said that Churchill was smoking a pipe on that occasion and not the customary cigar! When war ended, the Clyde-based barges rerigged and sailed south again via the Caledonian Canal and Inverness, calling at Aberdeen and other ports down the north-east coast on their way home.

By this time the sailing barge fleet was reduced by more than half, and when the Thames Barge Sailing Club was constituted in 1948 'to maintain one or more Thames sailing barges in commission in the London River', the number had dwindled to less than 200.

By 1963, the centenary year of the Thames race, the number of sailing barges had reached an all-time low and it was feared that the vessel would, in the space of a decade or so, become a thing of the past. A small fleet of motor barges was still trading, about a dozen vessels were rigged privately and sailing as yachts, and a number of others were providing cheap houseboat homes on the Thames and Medway and at east coast ports. The trust set up to run the *Memory* as a trading barge had failed and only the *Cambria*, under her owner–master Bob Roberts, was still working under sail alone. Then came the announcement that the famous Thames race was to be abandoned, and the lovely *Sara* and *Dreadnought*, last of the commercially owned racing barges, were to be scrapped.

However, the tide was beginning to turn and the barges did not disappear. Instead, as the 1970s approached, more and more people were becoming conservation-minded, and against the accelerating inflation in our national economy the mood was changing to sympathy with those seeking to preserve our national inheritance. Gradually more and more barges were restored and rerigged for sailing. A number of commercial companies became aware of the promotional and publicity value of these unique vessels. Private individuals saw the opportunity of running barges for holiday chartering. Out of the ashes of the *Memory* project rose the phoenix of the East Coast Sail Trust, which successfully runs the lovely coaster *Thalatta* as a school ship. Other trusts and even local authorities have sponsored barges as outward-bound and sail-training vessels. Barge racing has re-established itself and annual matches are now held on the Medway, Swale, Colne, Blackwater, Orwell and at Southend. Associations among the barge owners have been established to monitor the training of skippers and mates, and the qualifications so gained have been accepted by the Board of Trade.

Some forty to fifty barges are now in commission and a new generation of young skippers, such as Geoff Harris of the *Pudge*, are stepping successfully into the shoes of the old sailormen. It seems, then, that the future of the Thames spritsail barge and its colourful traditions is in safe hands and with the goodwill and enthusiasm of the devotees, the familiar tanned sails and varnished spreets will continue to grace our shores for many years to come.

Below: Competing barges, including *Pudge*, waiting to start the Pin Mill Race

4
THE GREAT
J-CLASS YACHTS
Ian Dear

When, in 1920, Sir Thomas Lipton failed to win back the America's Cup at his fourth attempt, many people must have thought he would give up trying. However, the 'Boating Grocer' was a determined man and in 1929 he challenged yet again. His perseverence was not rewarded, but in pursuing the 'auld mug', as he called it, for a fifth time he unwittingly helped create what has come to be accepted as the greatest class of yacht ever built: the Js.

The long gap between the two challenges was not caused by reluctance on either side to race. Sir Thomas was playing a waiting game for, in his opinion at least, the dice were loaded on the side of the Americans. Only the knowledge that the Cup would simply gather dust on its pedestal unless they improved the odds might persuade them to do something about it.

In this he proved correct, but the changes came slowly. In 1925 the North American Yacht Racing Union was founded and two years later it accepted, among other things, that all large yachts must conform to Lloyd's scantling rules. This was the breakthrough that Lipton had been hoping for, as a challenging yacht could now be built that was strong enough to sail across the Atlantic – one of the rules to which any challenger had to adhere – without meeting a defender which had been built with no such restrictions placed upon her.

The America's Cup had always been raced for by the biggest yachts that both countries could put in the water. But though they accepted Lloyd's scantlings for their larger yachts, the Americans continued to build them to the Universal Rule – drawn up by the famous American designer Nat Herreshoff – and not to the International Rule, to which British racing yachts had been designed since 1907. Knowing that a challenge from a yacht built to the International Rule would never be accepted, Lipton planned to have his latest challenger built to the Universal Rule – as his previous one, *Shamrock IV*, had been.

But in 1920 the competing yachts had both measured 75 feet on the waterline; this time, Lipton proposed a boat which would fit into one of the largest class of sloops that the defending club, the New York Yacht Club, possessed. Since 1896 the club had designated letters to each of its racing classes, and in 1929 this system was revised so that the sloop and yawl fleet was allotted the letters I to Q. Only one of the club's yachts was big enough to fall into the I-class, and then only just. However, two others fell into the J-class, which measured between 76 and 87 feet on the waterline, and it was within these limits that Lipton proposed building his new *Shamrock V*.

Though the end result was not dissimilar, the formulae for the two rules were quite different. Lipton's architect, Charles E. Nicholson, was therefore faced with designing a Cup challenger to a rule he hardly knew, and which *The New York Times* described in exasperation as 'worse than a Chinese puzzle or Professor Einstein's theory of relati-

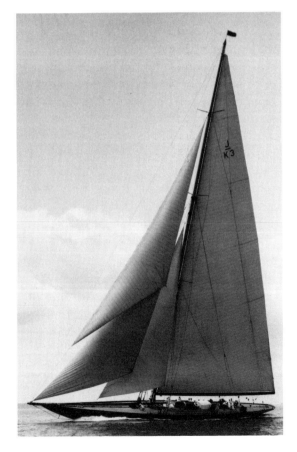

Left: *Shamrock V*, Sir Thomas Lipton's final challenger for the America's Cup and the first British J

vity'. To add to Nicholson's difficulties only one yacht was to be built, so there was no room for experimentation and no hope of the challenger having any meaningful trials against a similar opponent.

The Americans, on the other hand, built four potential defenders – *Enterprise, Weetamoe, Yankee* and *Whirlwind* – each of which was a different waterline length. They then raced them against one another until the best emerged. Curiously, the most successful, *Enterprise*, was the shortest, but the Js never conformed to the normal criteria as, under the Universal Rule, the greater the length the greater the displacement, while the sail area stayed more or less constant – a clear case of diminishing returns. When eventually the Js were constructed to the maximum possible length, it was because a larger base was needed for the hugely improved sails and rigging which had begun to appear. The fastest J that year was, in fact, *Weetamoe*, the second-smallest boat, but *Enterprise* was superbly skippered by Harold Vanderbilt who once again proved that the fastest boat is not always the best.

Besides having the most skilled America's Cup campaigner aboard her, *Enterprise* had a multitude of winches and a revolutionary duralumin mast that was two thirds the weight of a normal hollow wooden one. 'The mast is a miracle,' commented the designer of a rival J to Starling Burgess, the designer of *Enterprise*, 'and it is a miracle that you can keep it in the boat!' For the Americans at least, the age of technology had arrived in yachting.

Nicholson, an outstanding designer, did his best and produced a first-rate yacht that proved herself in the British regatta circuit of 1930 to be every bit as fast as any of her 'big boat' rivals. Out of the twenty-two races in which *Shamrock V* took part before sailing across the Atlantic for the Challenge, she won fifteen and came second in four. This gave rise to wild speculation about her chances of retrieving the America's Cup – though her record was not quite as brilliant as it appeared, for the handicappers at first under-rated her. She also possessed material advantages over her British rivals in having a hollow spar, no cabin fittings, and a centre board, none of which was allowed by British rules at the time. However, Lipton expressed himself well satisfied and by calling her *Shamrock V* carried on the tradition of christening all his challengers by this name. She was 81.7 feet on the waterline and had a 78-ton lead keel. She was of semi-composite construction for, though her frames were entirely of steel, her stem, stern-post and counter-timbers were made from teak, her planking was mahogany and her deck was laid with yellow pine. Her mast was no less than 162 feet from truck to heel and was constructed from fifty pieces of silver spruce.

However, although she was beautifully constructed, the British challenger still depended on the brawn of her professional crew, not on winches, and the whole campaign to retrieve the America's Cup was equally old-fashioned. Lipton knew nothing about sailing a yacht, or so he professed, and left the management of his new challenger in the hands of his representative, an amateur yachtsman called Duncan Neill, and the professional skipper, Ted Heard. It was a combination which worked well enough on the British regatta circuit, but it was totally inadequate when facing a man like Vanderbilt, who welded his crew into one working unit that had long ago discarded the British sporting attitude of 'gentlemen and players'. The result was disaster: *Shamrock V* did not win a race.

Lipton died in October of the following year, before he could issue yet another challenge. At the time of his death British yachting was already moving into a new era in which the amateur owner steered his own yacht and technological innovation was accepted and encouraged. But if Lipton represented a bygone age, he had, by introducing the Js to Britain, ensured that his name would be forever linked with the founding of a class now generally recognised as representing the pinnacle of yachting in Britain.

Only ten J-class yachts were ever built. Six were constructed in the United States by syndicates of rich men concerned solely with defending the America's Cup – which, even in those days, was a kind of holy grail for American yachtsmen. In Britain, on the other hand, the four Js that came to grace the waters of the Solent and elsewhere were not constructed for that reason alone. Indeed, one of them, *Velsheda*, never challenged and it was never intended that she should. Their value lay as much in the social prestige they gave their owners as in their ability to dominate the regatta circuit, which every summer took them to a number of towns and holiday resorts around the coast of Britain. No vulgar syndicates owned the British Js, but super-rich individuals who enjoyed the social ambience created and sustained by just one man: King George V.

It is arguable that the King loved his yachting even more than he did shooting, though his companions on the water were very different from those he mixed with on the grouse moor. The sport of yachting contained its fair share of the aristocracy, but none seems to have ventured into the rarified atmosphere of the 'big class' which was dominated,

Above: King George V at the wheel of his famous yacht *Britannia*, photographed with some of his crew about 1925

almost without exception, by those who had made their fortunes in industry. Even the Royal Yacht Squadron, a one-time bastion of the gentry, had been forced to accept the social revolution wrought by the First World War; and though it had stubbornly refused, until the eleventh hour, to elect Lipton, it had let others of lesser note through its august portals – as the following conversation, said to have taken place on the Squadron lawn, illustrates.

'Who owns that yacht over there?' a young American visitor, newly arrived from a United States in the grip of Prohibition, asked her host.

'Ernest Guinness', was the reply.

'What, the guy that makes the Guinness?'

Her host nodded.

'And that cute little black steam yacht?'

'That belongs to Richard Hennessy.'

'Hennessy's brandy?'

'The same family', her host replied.

'What about that big white ketch?' she asked, and was told it belonged to a family which made beer. The girl was incredulous.

'You say all those guys make hooch, yet they're members of the Yacht Squadron?'

Her host answered that that was the case.

'No kidding!' exclaimed the girl. 'And they told me this was a high-hat club!'

The 'beerocracy' did not in fact dominate the 'big class' either, though Hugh Paul, the owner of *Astra*, was a maltster. Two of its members, Tom Sopwith and Richard Fairey, had made their fortunes from manufacturing aeroplanes; Sir William Berry, later Lord Camrose, was a newspaper proprietor; Sir Howard Frank was an estate agent; and T. B. F. Davis, a great favourite of the King, was an ex-stevedore whose colourful language could be heard half-way across the Solent as he urged on the crew of his schooner *Westward*.

The truth is that the King probably liked this motley collection of yachtsmen around him and enjoyed competing against them. They must have presented a very different view of life from that of the blue-blooded courtiers who normally surrounded him. Perhaps the fact that Queen Mary loathed yachting and rarely accompanied him also had something to do with his affection for the sport. It can certainly be assumed that she had little time for her husband's fellow yachtsmen, for most of them, as the King was well aware, had been through the divorce courts.

'Why J?' the King is supposed to have asked a leading yachting journalist of the time when that letter first began to appear on the mainsails of the 'big class'. The journalist explained what the letter denoted.

'It should have been "A"', said the King with a glimmer of a smile after hearing the explanation.

'Why, Sir?' asked the journalist.

'"A" for adultery', the King replied with a chuckle. 'With the exception of old Davis, I'm the only owner in the class who still has his original wife!'

Whatever his motive, it was solely due to the King that the regatta circuit for the 'big boats' was resuscitated after the First World War, when he decided to recommission his famous yacht *Britannia*. Without his lead it is doubtful whether anyone else would have gone to the expense of building or recommissioning yachts such as *Lulworth*, *Westward*, *Candida*, *Astra*, *White Heather II* and *Cambria*, which were all racing in the regatta circuit when *Shamrock V* was launched in 1930. That summer, eight yachts of the 'big class' raced together. It must have been a wonderful sight, but it must also have caused the rule makers to pause for thought.

In fact, it must have given those deputed to run yacht racing in Britain a bad headache, because these eight yachts were the products of three quite separate classes. *Astra, Cambria* and *Candida* had been built to the revised International Rule of 1928; *Shamrock V*, of course, had been constructed to the American Universal Rule; and the rest were yachts of various shapes and sizes which had been lumped together and given different handicaps to ensure that they (especially *Britannia*) had good racing and a fair chance of winning prize money. It was, to put it bluntly, a pig's breakfast, and something had to be done about it.

What those in charge decided upon was a typical British compromise, and like most intelligent compromises it worked remarkably well. The Universal Rule, as represented by the four American Js and the one British J then in existence, had become an established fact. If the British were to challenge again, it was going to have to be with a J-class yacht, so it made obvious sense to abandon building yachts over 14½ metres to the 1928 International Rule and instead to adopt the Universal Rule for this type of cutter. However, to accept the Universal Rule in its entirety would be to ignore the 'big class' yachts already in existence, so it was decided to adopt the parts of the rule which suited these yachts and to ignore the rest. By doing this, all the yachts except the schooner *Westward* could be altered to fit the British version of the Universal Rule.

At the same time the Americans altered the rating rules for the J-class, so bringing them more into line with British thinking. Thus, in 1931, the regatta season was able to continue unhindered, the yachts' owners could go on using their boats for cruising as well as racing, and anyone who wanted to build a new J could do so knowing full well that he was not building a one-off, suitable only for an America's Cup challenge.

These alterations did cause casualties – *Enterprise* was considered too small to bear the new minimum mast weight, and the cost of converting *Lulworth* proved unacceptable to her owner – but on the whole the compromise worked well, and even *Westward* was somehow accommodated when she turned out to race, which she did with decreasing frequency. The King again led the way by being the first to announce that *Britannia* was to be altered to the new rules, and soon most of the other owners followed suit. Their decision to do so caused an upsurge of British interest in the 'big class' which is now legendary.

The 1931 season was in many ways an experimental one for the 'big boats' as they tried out their new rigs and other alterations. It was also blighted by the Depression, and not all the yachts raced in all the regattas. *Shamrock V*, however, did not miss one of the thirty-two starts and easily came top of the class with eighteen firsts and six seconds to her credit. Dear old Lipton must have been delighted.

The 'big boat' racing that summer must have been followed closely by a young aircraft millionaire, recently elected to the exclusive Royal Yacht Squadron and acknowledged as one of the top 12-metre helmsmen in the country. For when Lipton died, T.O.M. Sopwith decided to join the 'big class'. He bought *Shamrock V* with the aim of challenging for the America's Cup in the foreseeable future.

The 1932 season saw the entry of not only Sopwith into the 'big class' but also W. F. Stephenson, the chairman of Woolworth, who had bought *White Heather II* from Lord Waring and converted her to the J-class. Stephenson, though not a yachtsman, obviously enjoyed the rigours of racing, for that autumn, much to everyone's delight and surprise, he ordered a J-class yacht from Charles E. Nicholson, who had designed *Shamrock V*. He named her *Velsheda*, a combination of the first two or three letters of the Christian names of his three daughters, Velma, Sheila and Daphne, and soon afterwards a photograph appeared in a swank magazine of him at the helm of his new yacht with his daughter Sheila standing beside him, complete with sailor's cap and teddy bear tucked under her left arm. Having acquired a J-class yacht, he must have thought the *ensemble* would be incomplete without a steam yacht, because he bought one of those too, naming her *Malahne*, which conveniently used up the remaining letters in his daughters' names. A bit of a throwback was Stephenson, to the days when owners could not even recognise their own yachts and employed professional skippers to race them as others did jockeys at Epsom and Goodwood. But by all accounts he learnt quickly and was a very charming fellow.

Unlike *Shamrock V*, *Velsheda* was made entirely of steel – the first yacht to be so constructed in England since 1913 – and was 83 feet on the waterline. This being a time of economic disaster, Stephenson had *White Heather II* broken up and to save money, used what he could of her in his new boat. Nevertheless, *Velsheda* was in no way skimped and during the 1933 season proved herself to be very fast indeed. Despite having to give *Shamrock V* 3.6 seconds per mile, *Britannia* 4.8 seconds and *Astra* as much as 5.4 seconds, she topped the class with twenty wins, ten seconds and a third out of forty-three starts, consistently beating *Shamrock V*, a much improved yacht since 1930.

If Sopwith had ever had any idea of challenging for the America's Cup with *Shamrock V*, he must have abandoned it that summer, for she only managed to come fourth behind the amazing *Britannia* (now forty years old) and the smaller *Astra*. So as soon as the season finished, Sopwith sold his J to fellow aeroplane manufacturer Richard Fairey – who renamed her simply *Shamrock* – ordered a new J from Charles E. Nicholson and issued his challenge through the Royal Yacht Squadron to the New York Yacht Club for a series of races off Newport in 1934. He would have challenged a year earlier but had been advised by the King, who as Admiral of the Royal Yacht Squadron had to keep an eye on such matters, that a challenge at that time would have been construed as untimely because of the severe economic climate. The NYYC were not too happy to receive it for 1934 either, and they had great difficulty finding a potential defender, though in the end Vanderbilt stepped into the breach and put up most of the money for a new yacht himself.

With Sopwith's new yacht, Charles E. Nicholson came as close to producing the perfect J as he was able – that is to say, very close indeed. Although his achievement did not quite match that of Olin Stephens and Starling Burgess with *Ranger* in 1937, Nicholson certainly came a lot closer to perfection than Burgess did with *Rainbow*, the 1934 American defender.

Sopwith named his new yacht *Endeavour* and had her hull painted blue (one yachting journalist called her his Darling Jade). She was full of inventive touches. Sopwith's right-hand man, aeronautical engineer Frank Murdoch, not only provided him with bar rigging but also such refinements as wind-direction and speed indicators, 'rowing' winches with which a 2-ton strain could be set up, and an improved Park Avenue boom, a triangular-shaped spar which shaped the foot of the mainsail to maximum efficiency. *Endeavour* also had an ace up her sleeve in the shape of a double-clewed jib called a quadrilateral. Unfortunately, it was hoisted during one of the yacht's trial races in the Solent and appeared a very short time later on the other side of the Atlantic, where it was called, more picturesquely, a Greta Garbo.

Unlike the unfortunate *Shamrock, Endeavour* had a useful trial horse in the shape of *Velsheda* and an owner who was one of the best helmsmen in the business. As a brilliant aircraft designer, Sopwith

Opposite: W. F. Stephenson's steel J-class *Velsheda* in her heyday

knew all about aerodynamics and stress factors, and along with Murdoch he applied this knowledge to *Endeavour*'s rigging with good effect.
There is little doubt that the British challenger was as well tuned as she
could be, and that she showed herself to be a very fast boat indeed. Of
the twelve races she took part in before leaving for Newport, she won
nine and came second in three. Sopwith's campaign also had an air of
professionalism and confidence about it that not only raised the hopes of
the British but cast some gloom among the American camp, who were
struggling with a yacht launched late and which was not as fast as she
should have been. After fourteen challenges and the passing of eighty-
three years, was the 'auld mug' at last going to recross the Atlantic?

It could have happened – perhaps one might even be permitted to say
it *should* have – but it never came to pass. The main reason has been
well documented, though what lay behind it has never been fully
revealed. Even Vanderbilt openly admitted afterwards that the blue-
hulled *Endeavour* was the faster boat, but Sopwith had management
problems that, with hindsight, stymied his chances of winning before
he even crossed the Atlantic. His paid crew, under the professional
skipper George Williams, could handle the huge cutter with tremendous skill, and a trained and experienced team was essential to get
the best out of her. Yet there must have been an underlying tension
between the crew and the yacht's owner, because a few days before
Endeavour was due to leave for America the paid hands struck for
higher wages.

Rightly or wrongly, Sopwith refused to negotiate a deal. Instead, he
dismissed the strikers – some of the more reactionary yachting magazine editors went so far as to call them 'mutineers' – and took on not
other paid hands but a number of eager amateurs rounded up for him by
Olympic gold-medallist Christopher Boardman. Boardman and
another amateur crew member, Beecher Moore, had been given berths
aboard *Shamrock* that summer, so they knew something about crewing
aboard a J. Many years later Moore wrote a telling article about his
experience on the *Shamrock*, perhaps revealing the crux of what went
wrong with Sopwith's challenge. 'We found,' he commented, 'when we
got on board the boat that it was very much like a well-run country
house in that the gentleman does not go into the kitchen and on a
well-run J-class the owner does not go forward of the mast. So while all
the theory in the world was at Fairey's fingertips, when it came to
actually sailing he didn't know that the foresail backed the jib almost all
the way round the course.'

Certainly Sopwith would have known this, as one of the outstanding yachtsmen of his generation, but the atmosphere on *Endeavour* would not have been dissimilar to that which pervaded *Shamrock*. That was how yachting was conducted in the 'big class' during the 1930s. The owner might now be the helmsman with the professional skipper relegated to the position of mate, but the owner and those who helped him on the afterdeck, the afterguard, were definitely still the 'gentlemen' while the rest of the crew were the 'players'. So it is not surprising that Sopwith emphasised to Boardman that he only required men who did what they were told; he did not want his yacht filled with a crew who constantly offered their advice – even if they *were* Olympic gold-medallists.

In the event, this is just what he got. According to Boardman, however, the amateur crew could probably have offered Sopwith better advice than he received from his afterguard, who, with the exception of Frank Murdoch, were worse than useless. The navigator, for instance, a Merchant Navy officer, though competent at deep-sea navigation was of doubtful merit when it came to sailing around an America's Cup course. In fact, he proved to be so bad that *Rainbow*'s navigator was provoked to remark that 'there were times at which we wondered if anyone were navigating for *Endeavour* at all'.

During the crucial third race, with *Endeavour* 2–0 up, the challenger was well ahead when Sherman Hoyt, at the wheel of the defending yacht, lured Sopwith into tacking unnecessarily to cover him when Sopwith could have, in fact, sailed straight for the finishing line. The weather was misty, the wind so light as to be almost non-existent, and the only conclusion Hoyt could reach was that *Endeavour*'s navigator had not known exactly where the finishing line was!

This race seemed to break the will of the challenger, and it certainly gave new heart to the Americans, who went on to win the series 4-2. The fourth race proved equally controversial, and after the series Sopwith declared that he would never challenge again.

The bad atmosphere in which the fifteenth challenge ended ironically had a very positive effect on the 'big class'. The following year Gerard Lambert, the American owner of *Yankee*, decided that he had better try to patch up the rift in Anglo-American yachting relations by bringing his own J across the Atlantic to take part in that summer's British regatta circuit.

If the J-class era is now regarded as the sublime decade of British yachting, the summer of 1935 was the peak of those halcyon years. It

Above: *Yankee* **winning her first race of the 1935 British season, at Southend**

had taken five long years to reach this summit of perfection – but the slope down the other side was very steep indeed . . .

However, no one was to know at the beginning of that memorable season that the Js had only two more years' racing ahead of them. Those 'big boats' that had been converted to the class were sailing at their best; there were no fewer than four genuine Js in hot competition with one another; an American yacht was racing in British waters for the first time in decades; the King was still alive and well, and it was his Jubilee year; and, *Britannia*, though now outclassed however kindly the handicappers might look upon her, was still racing. If the weather held up, it was going to be a year that no one forgot in a hurry.

It is perhaps necessary to pause at this point in the apparently all-too-short history of the Js to mention that the five years of their existence had seen many improvements in their rigging and sails. Metal masts and a double-headed foresail rig were now *de rigueur*, and gone were the old hollow wooden sticks with the old-fashioned triple fore-sails. In 1934 *Yankee* had even tried one large genoa but without much success. However, parachute spinnakers were well established, as was bar rigging which was able to take the tremendous strains on the mast with much greater efficiency.

The loftiness of the masts of the J-class, which was dictated by the Universal Rule, gave the Js a high aspect ratio rig that maximised the use of the sail area allowed. But it also made them vulnerable, and Js on both sides of the Atlantic soon became increasingly prone to breaking masts. Already, and too often for the liking of followers of the British regatta circuit – for it *was* a spectator sport – one yacht or another would not race because there was either too much or too little wind. So prevalent did this become in 1935, when seven races were cancelled because of high winds, that the story began to go around that a skipper knew if he would be able to race the next day by putting a lighted candle on deck before turning in. If it was still alight in the morning, it showed there was not enough wind to race; if it was not, then there was too much!

In fact, the 'big boats' had always regularly lost spars. But there was something in the argument of the old tars that yachts were not as seaworthy as they had been in the days of the gaff rig, the overhanging boom, and massive – and massively inefficient – clouds of canvas; and it should be added that when the Js crossed the Atlantic, they were sometimes towed and always had a smaller rig. Armchair critics also had a point when they warned that the huge expense of running the Js and continually trying to improve them would, in the end, prove self-defeating. 'Are J-class too large?' one yachting magazine headline queried, adding ominously that, the racing was 'now at its zenith'.

However, these seeds of doubt had hardly been sown at the beginning of the 1935 season. It started with a bang when, during the second regatta, at Southend, *Endeavour*'s mast went over the side – the first time this had happened to a J – and *Shamrock*'s flexible boom snapped. Worst of all, *Astra*'s steward was catapulted overboard while trying to control the spinnaker sheet in the half-gale conditions and was lost in one of the very few fatal accidents the 'big class' ever sustained.

Yankee won that race, giving the Americans a timely boost to their confidence. Totally unbalanced by the loss of her mast, *Endeavour* moved so violently that her crew had to crawl around on their hands and knees. It looked to others as if the Americans had put them there and that *Yankee* was going to sweep the board. For the British it was an

Above: *Endeavour* being towed in after her mishap at Southend, 1935

inauspicious start, but the fickleness of the wind on many occasions that summer, plus the tricks of the tide, a permanent factor in British yachting, were both unknown factors to the Americans and soon made the racing neck-and-neck.

Lambert was both puzzled and amused by the eccentricity of the English yacht-racing scene. He wrote in his book *Yankee in England*:

> The race at Dover on 10 June initiated us in the odd method of starting English races, which is so different from the system in this country [the USA]. Our starting instructions read that when a certain lamp post on the end of a certain breakwater came in line with the east edge of the tower of St Mary's church, we would be on the range, adding as an afterthought that there would be a stake boat a quarter of a mile offshore, but that it had nothing to do with the line. Reading these instructions impressed me with the fact that to succeed in racing in England one must have a knowledge of lamp posts (possibly from nocturnal prowlings) and a thorough familiarity with eccelesiastical architecture.

Another aspect of the yachting scene that never ceased to amaze Lambert was the fact that in the West Country the courses were often arranged specifically with spectators in mind. 'We had heard that these great racing contraptions often came into inner harbours and out again and around several times for the amusement of the public, but we could scarcely believe our eyes when we saw them actually do it.'

The West Country regattas had their own very special flavour, though hardly staged with the professionalism the Americans must have been used to at home. For one thing, the mark boats had a habit of being in the wrong place, or shifting their moorings even while a race was underway. During one foggy race one was found motoring home, and when hailed by a competing J the crew replied that they hadn't seen a yacht all day and did not propose to wait any longer!

The Torbay regattas would be conducted from the decks of a Brix-ham trawler complete with an ancient starting gun. The proceedings were obviously as hilarious as they were confusing, as one yachting correspondent amusingly conveyed:

> Smoke now wreathed the trawler, as in some desperate Napoleonic sea-fight; and it is to be feared that there were moments when the race officials were hard put to it to keep up with the pace of events. Every five minutes and every ten minutes a class must receive its guns, and at the same intervals its five-minute and starting flags. Flags! we were draped, festooned, and garlanded with them; flags of all nations, and the International Code, flags of local historical significance, and flags of such faded colouring and esoteric design that there could be no knowing whether they had any significance at all. And yet beneath and between all this smother of bunting you might have seen, as I once saw, a deckchair occupied by an elderly gentleman in a white suit, panama-hatted, working at *The Times* crossword with a gold pencil. The Deputy Lord-Lieutenant, no doubt.

After racing at Dover, in the Solent, at Plymouth and in a special regatta at Le Havre – 'The racing in France is rubbish,' commented one old sea-dog, 'but the girls are charming' – the 'big boats' took part in Cowes Week before once again sailing for the West Country. The last regatta of the season was at Dartmouth and *Yankee* needed to win one more race to end the season level-pegging with *Endeavour*. Better and closer competition could not have been imagined.

The racing the previous day had been cancelled, but on that final morning the committee decided to let the yachts start. Both *Astra* and *Candida*, however, thought it too great a risk to compete. The wind was blowing between 25 and 30 knots, and though the sea was not as rough as it had been, there was a nasty chop that put the lee rails of the yachts awash. The first leg was a close reach, the next a run, and at the West Skerries buoy, which marked the turn for the start of the second leg, *Yankee* was leading, with *Endeavour, Velsheda* and *Shamrock* tucked safely away astern and to leeward. Lambert, in a winning mood, was at the wheel and he had his skipper standing by to help him jibe at the mark. He was holding the yacht off slightly to cut the buoy as closely as possible when there was a grinding, crunching noise, the like of which he had never heard before. He lifted his eyes and saw *Yankee*'s 156-foot mast crumple and fall overboard. The others, seeing the American in distress, lowered their sails and abandoned the race.

Thus ended *Yankee*'s season in British waters; and it ended too, in all probability, the invincibility of the Js in the eyes of the *cognoscenti*. From then on many were openly critical, not only because of their lack of seaworthiness but also because of their size.

That autumn Sopwith sold *Endeavour*, proposed a challenge for the following year and announced that he was having a new J built – *Endeavour II*. At the same time his great yachting and business rival, Richard Fairey, announced that he also intended to challenge, not with a J but in the smaller K-class, and there were many who supported the prospect of decreasing, if only slightly, the size of challenger and defender. However, his challenge was not accepted, while Sopwith's was delayed until 1937 because of the 1936 American presidential elections.

If Fairey's challenge had been accepted, would it have saved the 'big class' from extinction? It is unlikely, as what really killed those huge and beautiful cutters was the death of George V in January 1936. Soon afterwards, on instructions left in his will, *Britannia* was scuttled, and down with her went the hopes and memories of a generation of yachtsmen, both professional and amateur. The racing that season was a shadow of what it had been, and at Plymouth both *Endeavour II* and *Velsheda* were dismasted. 'When the winds of July and August blow,' someone recited unkindly, 'the masts of most of the J-class go'; and at a conference during Cowes Week later that year the Yacht Racing Association issued a statement that they were investigating the possibility of introducing the L-class, which had a maximum length of 56 feet. How are the mighty fallen! Two months later a yachting journalist commented tartly that if anybody had published a kind word about the Js in the yachting press anywhere it had escaped *his* notice. He was right: they hadn't.

In 1937, in the hope of finding more wind at Newport in midsummer, Sopwith asked that the America's Cup races take place in July and this was agreed. He therefore sailed *Endeavour II* across the Atlantic before the English regatta season began, and also took the original *Endeavour* with him (chartered for £1) as a trial horse. Gutted of its two best competitors, and with *Candida* already on the market, the 'big class' never appeared in 1937. After the America's Cup races, in which Sopwith was trounced by the super-J *Ranger*, the Americans were all invited to race in the regatta circuit in 1938, but none took up the invitation, and again the 'big class' did not appear.

Then came the Second World War, and the Js and yachting and all the excitement and frivolity of the regatta circuit were forgotten. Those American Js that had not yet been broken up were sent to the scrapyards to provide metal for the war industry – all except *Yankee*. She too was scrapped, but Lambert sent the money he received to Queen Mary, to be used at her discretion in the London hospitals. He sent it, he said, in memory of the courtesies shown *Yankee* by the King and herself: a nice touch with which to end the history of a great yachting class.

Yet this was not quite the end of the story for the J-class. There are still a few of the 'big boats' about, and the American owner of one of them is determined that we shall see them sailing together again. Elizabeth Meyer is working to restore *Endeavour* in time to launch her for the summer of 1987. 'What I would dearly love to see', she wrote in the autumn of 1985, 'is a few of these old beauties – say *Velsheda, Astra, Shamrock* and *Endeavour* – all on the New York Yacht Club Cruise, "racing up Buzzard's Bay on the afternoon sou'wester". I think it will happen.'

Below (left to right): *Yankee*, *Shamrock*, *Velsheda*, *Astra* **and** *Endeavour*, **1935**

A decade ago this would have seemed a fantasy, but now it looks just possible. There were even rumours in 1979, when the French were preparing for the 1980 challenge for the America's Cup – now sailed for in the comparatively tiny 12-metre-class yachts – that if Baron Bich, the French challenger, won, he would try to revive the J-class. It is highly unlikely that he would have succeeded, but the dream of *Endeavour*'s owner is well within the bounds of possibility. *Velsheda* has already been restored and is sailing with her original J-class sail plan after lying for many years in a mud berth on the Hamble river. *Astra*, too, is a possible candidate for Miss Meyer's dream, as her Italian owner has given her an extensive refit which includes her original sail plan.

Some of the other 'big boats' that used to race in the regatta circuit during the heyday of the Js have also miraculously survived the intervening years, but they are not such likely candidates for that race in Buzzard's Bay. *Cambria* is still afloat but as a cruising yacht, as is *Candida*, now ketch-rigged. *Lulworth*, although she was never converted to the J-class, is also going to be refitted but, like the other two, as a cruising ketch.

Shamrock has also been completely rejuvenated. After the War she turned up in the Mediterranean, where so many large yachts spend their twilight years, and there she steadily deteriorated until bought by an Italian businessman. In the mid-1970s, he commissioned her original builders, Camper & Nicholson, to refit her as a cruising yacht, but also to restore her appearance to as close to the original as possible. The task cost around £1 million and was carried out to the highest standards of workmanship. She was stripped to her frames, replanked in teak and given luxurious accommodation while still retaining the original bird's-eye maple panelling in the saloon and elsewhere. She was then rerigged as a cutter and her 152-foot aluminium mast made her almost a J-class yacht once again, but not quite. The extra equipment aboard, plus two powerful diesel engines, increased her waterline length from 81 to 84 feet and her displacement from 134 to 150 tons. So, though a beautiful yacht once more, she would hardly be a match for the 'Darling Jade', *Endeavour*. Yet ten years ago I was convinced that neither *Velsheda* nor *Endeavour* would ever sail again, so I hope to be proved wrong once more. Dear old Lipton would surely be delighted if I were.

5
OLD GAFFERS FOR EVER

Robert Simper

The summer of 1985 was one of gales and heavy rain. The bad weather conditions ruined the plans of many sailing people around the coast of Britain, but the strong winds gave one group a wonderful race. This was the East Coast Old Gaffers' Race, sailed from the River Blackwater in Essex, one of the largest and most attractive traditional boat events in Britain in which no two boats are the same and the whole estuary is dotted with white and brown sails of every shade. Yet it is more than this: it is a stubborn reminder of a breed of sailing craft which has refused to die out and is in fact making something of a comeback.

If one glances back through the pages of old yachting magazines, it is noticeable that boats are described as cutters, sloops, ketches and so on, according to their rig. The word 'gaff' is never used because everyone knew that virtually every craft was gaff, whether cutter, sloop or ketch, and there was thus no need to include this extra description. The gaff sail is a four-sided sail set fore and aft (that is, down the central line of the hull) with a spar known as the gaff supporting it at the head (top) of the sail. The gaff sail became popular in the eighteenth century because it was a highly versatile rig which gave the best all-round performance at every point of sailing and was superior for going to windward (sailing into the wind).

The Royal Navy started using the gaff cutter rig in its dispatch craft because it enabled the vessels to reach the fleet whatever the weather conditions. The Revenue Service also adopted the cutter in its long and bloody war with the smuggling gangs. The huge luggers used by the smugglers, particularly in the English Channel, were actually faster on some points of sailing, but the cutters had to have superior all-round performance to seek out the prey before the chase could ever begin.

In the early nineteenth century, the Revenue cutters were regarded as the fastest of all the British fore-and-aft-rigged craft. However, the war with the smugglers was never won at sea, and it was not until the late 1820s that the British government managed to form an effective

Above: The restored gaff-rigged bawley *Helen & Violet*, first launched in 1906

coast guard service which fought and won that particular battle on land. Even so, the Revenue cutters were admired and copied by fishermen, pilots and yachtsmen all along the British coast. The single-masted cutter grew so popular that it became known as the national rig of Britain, and even today the vast majority of craft using gaff sails are still cutters.

The nineteenth century saw continuous industrial expansion which brought about a growth in the number of coastal sailing craft. Increased trade created a demand for more trading vessels, and the expanding population presented a growing market for fish, resulting in huge fleets of smacks, all gaff-rigged, based at such ports as Brixham, Lowestoft, Yarmouth, Hull, Grimsby and many more. In addition, the wealth generated by industry financed yacht racing in huge schooners and cutters, often over 100 feet long and virtually all with gaff sails. These were crewed by paid hands, usually drawn from the fishing community during the summer months.

The golden age of the gaff rig was from about 1880 to 1914. Many superb types of work boat were evolved in this period within the regional traditions of Britain, while on the yachting scene men of wealth invested unlimited amounts of gold sovereigns in trying to build the fastest yacht. Whenever owners met in their elite yacht clubs, they happily grumbled that a yacht was nothing more than a hole in the water to pour money into, yet they still went on commissioning new designs from the building yards of the Solent, Essex and the Clyde.

Yacht racing in Britain began on the Thames when King Charles II returned from exile in Holland and brought with him a 'yacht' given to him by the VOC (Dutch East India Company) in 1660. The King and his friends started racing the same way they raced horses in that they bet heavily on matches between two boats. The first record of an event recognisable as a proper yacht race took place on the Thames in 1749, but there were no club-organised races until the forming of the Cumberland Fleet in London in 1775. The Thames remained the centre of yachting until the mid-Victorian period, by which time that great river was becoming increasingly dirty and congested as London grew into the world's largest port at the centre of a mighty empire. Yachtsmen, fed up with having their races interrupted by steamers and bargemen, made use of the new-fangled railways and travelled to the Solent to continue their sport there.

Cowes then became the focal point of yachting. The Royal Yacht Squadron established itself in Cowes Castle overlooking the entrance to the River Medina, while Queen Victoria had a superb view of the Solent from her beloved Osborne House nearby. When the New York schooner *America* came over in 1851 and won a race round the Isle of Wight for the Royal Yacht Squadron Cup, now known as the America's Cup, it is reported that Queen Victoria was 'not amused' at such Yankee cheek. This race, probably the most famous ever sailed by gaff yachts, resulted in the building of a whole series of truly beautiful craft in fabulously expensive attempts to win back the Cup. I once saw the famous Cup in its honoured place in the New York Yacht Club and was told that if it were ever lost, it would be replaced by the head of the guy that lost it! I have not dared to go back to see what filled the space after the Australians won the America's Cup.

Queen Victoria gave yachting royal approval, but it was her son, King Edward VII, who had what is considered to be the finest gaff racing yacht ever built. This was the *Britannia*, designed by George Watson of Glasgow and built by Hendersen in 1893. This royal yacht was only intended as a day racer round the buoys, yet by modern standards she was vast. The hull was 122 feet long, she set 10,300 square feet of sail and had a 90-foot mainboom. She required a paid crew of thirty to sail her, for in those days the owner and his guests seldom took part in the handling of the yacht at all.

The yacht owner decided where he wanted to go and the yacht skipper and crew (usually the skipper's friends and relations from his home village) sailed the yacht there. Sometimes, when racing, an owner would appoint a gentleman with a knowledge of the sea to be sailing master. His job was to advise the skipper on local conditions and to keep him to the niceties of the racing rules. Since the skippers and their crews kept the prize money, they raced to win and were not too bothered about 'sportsmanship'.

Occasionally a gentleman was actually at the wheel of his yacht during a race. There is no doubt that yacht owners such as Sir William Burton were talented and capable helmsmen, but the presence of an amateur at the wheel was bitterly resented by some paid hands: gentlemen were expected to know their place and leave the sailing to professionals.

Of all the great gaff yachts, *Britannia* was the favourite of the public, especially when the King's nephew, the German Emperor Wilhelm II, started racing with yachts called *Meteor* and for a few years before the First World War, Britain and Germany fought out their national rivalry in summer boat races.

There was so much publicity about the huge yachts and large numbers of paid hands that it was assumed that all yachtsmen were very rich and belonged to snobbish clubs. In fact, there were also less well known, purely local events sailed by men and a few women who were neither titled nor rich. Racing started on the Thames, but it quickly spread along the east coast. Woodbridge in Suffolk, for instance, had its first recorded yacht race in 1783 when the *Templer* and *Flora* raced 7 miles down the River Deben and back for a 'valuable silver cup'. The race received some publicity because afterwards, no doubt while the crews were celebrating, someone stole one of the craft. This did not stop the first regatta being organised at Woodbridge the following year, when Maldon had its first regatta, and Ipswich started one in 1791. On the south coast, regattas were held at Cowes and Southampton and similar local events were started along the south Devon coast. These early events seem to have been accompanied by drinking and betting rather than the pure sportsmanship of good clean races.

Organised races by yacht clubs were a nineteenth century development. The Deben Yacht Club at Woodbridge, formed in 1838, was a very early provincial club. By the end of the century most ports had an annual race for local fishermen and pilots in their work boats and in some places, such as the north-west of England and the Firth of Forth, industrial workers were regularly racing their own craft. All were very far removed from the huge cutters racing round the Solent and Clyde under a cloud of canvas, but even in the Victorian era sailing was a leisure activity of the ordinary man in the street.

Yachting and messing about in boats continued to grow in popularity, but the universal use of the gaff sail was challenged by the triangular marconi mainsail set on a very tall mast. This new rig was developed on the eastern seaboard of the United States about 1916 and introduced to Britain in the 1920s. Here it was called the bermudan rig and soon became very popular for racing. The smaller sail area resulted in a lower handicap and its facility for sailing closer to the wind meant the new rig was better for going fast forward. However, the very tall mast proved rather prone to breaking, so cruising yachtsmen stuck to their gaff sails because they were safer for long passages. After the Second World War, the safety of the bermudan rig was improved and it became as safe as gaff. By the late 1950s most yachts were being converted to the bermudan rig and very few new gaff boats were being built. Suddenly, after nearly two centuries of existence as the top rig for small craft, the gaff sail seemed doomed to extinction – just like the Viking longship, the Elizabethan galleon and countless other types which had vanished from the seas when their usefulness appeared at an end.

When I was looking for my first boat in 1957, however, I could not bring myself to buy a modern bermudan yacht but deliberately chose one (*Sea Fever*) with a gaff sail. This was on the east coast of England, where there has always been a healthy suspicion of anything new. There was by then plenty of secondhand gaff gear around, enabling gaff boats to be kept up quite cheaply, and this meant the bermudan yachts did not completely conquer the yachting scene.

Down on the south coast the gaff yachts were even further along the line to extinction when, in 1958, John Clarke (*Mareska*), Alec Rangabe (*Collina*) and Mike Richardson (*Betty*) met at the Jolly Sailor pub at Bursledon. They all agreed that there was no point in racing in local events with their gaff yachts because their large mainsails and the huge foretriangle measurements created by their bowsprits were given too large a handicap when racing compared to bermudan boats with smaller sails. Commiserating over drinks, the three hit upon the idea of holding a private race for gaff-sailed boats only. As the rig was then considered outdated, they decided to call it the Old Gaffers Race.

The first Solent Old Gaffers Race was sailed on 27 June 1959 from the Hamble river, out round a mark boat in Southampton Water and back for a social meeting at the RAF Yacht Club at Hamble in the evening. No records were kept and the whole event was very informal, but it developed into an annual race open to all gaffers. Each of the three original founders of the race had claimed that his boat was the fastest and all three won a race, thus not proving anything but establishing that there was still a vast amount of fun to be had sailing a gaff boat, even if it was out of fashion. The race got keen and loyal support from people such as Fiona Beale with *Devon Maid*, a smart 30-foot gaff yawl built in 1914 as a gentleman's Southampton day boat and one of the hundreds of obscure types of craft which would have been abandoned and forgotten had not the Old Gaffers Races been started.

On the east coast the fishing smack races at West Mersea and Maldon were revived after the Second World War for smacks sailed for pleasure. These were keenly fought local affairs, sometimes ending with heated rows in the pubs afterwards. Roy Clarkson, who sailed in these races with his smack *Fly*, wanted to start a race with a fixed form of handicap. John Scarlett, who lived in Maldon, became involved and called a meeting at his house. I went along and was delighted to meet a few people who were actually proud of their gaff boats. At this meeting we all agreed to start an East Coast Old Gaffers Race. The year was 1963. John Scarlett insisted on being secretary and my diary records that he had 'got everything worked out' – and so, it went on.

I volunteered to approach boat owners to take part, but this proved to be a rather depressing duty because I was told that we were a band of

Opposite: *Dorothy*, a Colchester fishing smack, sailing in the Orwell

cranks and the sooner the useless gaff died out, the better. Besides, the idea was quite mad – it was utterly impossible to handicap so many vastly different types of boats in a fair way. The smack owners would not even discuss the subject and it was implied that they would not race with mere yachts.

Undeterred we carried on, all determined that our East Coast Old Gaffers Race should not be just another race round the buoys. We saw ourselves as tough cruising sailors and insisted that it had to be a proper passage race. For the first race from Osea Island in the River Blackwater up the coast to Harwich we expected six boats to enter, but no fewer than thirty turned up, including smacks, and it seemed that we had filled a gap in the yachting scene. Unfortunately, the actual race was a flop because it took place on a delightful summer's day with not a breath of wind and most of the boats got no further than the Colne Bar. On corrected time the *Fanny* won, followed by *Fly*, and the schooner *Lora* was third. The others to finish were *Kestrel, Henriette Corista* and *Raymerswale*.

Mike Peyton, the cartoonist, raced with his cutter *Sugar Creek* and finally made it into Harwich Harbour in the early hours of the morning. His crew were tired and wanted to take a short cut inside a buoy to end the ordeal, but he insisted on sailing the whole course correctly. Mike finally finished and is still very proud of competing in the first race. Since then he has had three new gaff yachts built according to his own very progressive ideas which he asked the Burnham yacht designer Alan Hills to draw up. The boats, built in ferro-cement, have just one main halliard instead of the normal two.

The first race proved that the coastal passage course was impractical, but it was reported on Anglia Television and in the national press. Its existence was picked up by John Clarke of the Solent Old Gaffer Race (we had, after all, pirated their name!) and he wrote suggesting that the south and east coast races should link up to form the Old Gaffers Association. This duly came into being in the autumn of 1963.

Our object in founding this body was a little starry-eyed, for we wanted to be a worldwide organisation with the aim of bringing the gaff rig back into fashion. In 1963 that seemed a little unlikely, so we concentrated on creating an association for people who did not want to talk about modern techniques and bermudan yachts, but about traditional gaff boats.

At that time no one had any clear idea just how many gaff-sailed boats remained in Britain. We did know that many small gaff boats were not registered and their history and data were totally unrecorded. In addition, many former working craft were scattered far from their original home ports. Our survey of gaff boats took some years, but gradually every boat was given an OGA number and many now proudly display this on their mainsail, sometimes even with the OGA 'pitchfork' symbol (it is actually supposed to be a jaw where the gaff meets the mast!).

Most of the fishing craft which had been able to retain their fishing register numbers were not given an OGA number. The OGA numbers are allocated to identify craft in the future and of course to allow recognition of each boat in the races. New owners are usually interested in the history of their craft, and so far the OGA has gathered the history and data on about 1300 craft. In 1980 the Association's Register of Gaff-Rigged Boats was published and Dick and Pat Dawson are now adding corrections and additions to this unique record of some of Britain's smaller historical craft.

The oldest gaff-rigged craft still sailing is the 30-foot Essex smack *Boadicea*, which was built at Maldon in 1808. Like so many really old boats, she has been rebuilt several times and in 1970 all her timbers were renewed, but she still has the hull shape of a working vessel constructed while Europe was dominated by Napoleon. The *Boadicea* was an estuary oyster dredger, which meant that her hull was not subjected to the same strain as a seagoing craft. The Solent smacks or Itchen Ferries were similar inshore oyster boats, and I remember one called *Morning Star*, which dated from 1857, sailing in the early East Coast Old Gaffers Races. Unfortunately, she was burnt in 1980 at a boatyard near Portsmouth.

Another ancient Solent smack is the 27-foot *Sorella*, built in 1858 by the well-known local builder Dan Hatcher. Local legend has it that she was built for an army officer to race, but in about 1890 a fisherman bought her, sawed off the counter stern to give her a transom stern, and used her for fishing from the Hamble. Chris Waddington bought this little old-timer as an abandoned hulk and totally rebuilt her. He also owns the 42-foot gaff cutter *Moya*, which was constructed on the lines of a Morecambe Bay prawner by Crossfield Brothers at Arnside in 1910.

A small group of Itchen Ferries have survived from about the same period. The 19-foot *Wonder*, built by Hatcher in 1860, is usually to be seen at the Shamrock Quay, Southampton. The 18-foot *Flutt* and the 21-foot *Nellie*, both dating from 1865, are also rumoured to be still active on the Solent. The *Black Bess* of 1870 was based at Fishbourne, Isle of Wight, the last time I heard of her, but the one which has strayed the farthest from home is the 22-foot *Fanny*, built at Cowes in 1872.

The *Fanny* was used to transport oysters across to the mainland but, like many of these little Solent smacks, she was built very much with racing in mind and competed keenly for prize money in local regattas. After the Second World War, *Fanny* was lying abandoned in a south coast boatyard as no one in the progressive world of Solent racing had any use for this little Victorian cutter. David Cook of Ipswich found her and sailed her round to Pin Mill where he raced her with considerable success, even coming fifth out of forty in the Harwich–Ostend Race. When the East Coast Old Gaffers Race started, it was hardly surprising that *Fanny* won – and she went on to win again in 1964, 1965, 1967, 1968, 1969 and 1970. In order to achieve this continuing success, David Cook constantly introduced more modern equipment to the vessel, so that in the end she no longer looked like a traditional Itchen Ferry. The changes included replacing the rather square-cut mainsail with a modern high-cut peak mainsail. This proved more effective when reefed in strong winds, and he also put all the ballast inside. All these changes were made before 1970, whereas the trend among owners of traditional boats nowadays is not to try to turn them into modern craft, but to get them back to their original appearance. It is often found that the original sail plan works just as well as or even better than so-called improvements.

Most of the few boats which still survive from the 1870s are work boats such as the 42-foot *Madcap*, one of the famous Bristol Channel pilot cutters which are regarded as the most seaworthy of all the smaller sailing work boats. At least one yacht, the *Foam*, which was launched at Ilfracombe in 1876, appears to be still sailing. Quite why some boats last so long is a mystery. The 42-foot shrimping bawley *Band of Hope*, which Maurice Bailey has regularly sailed in the East Coast Old Gaffers Races, was built at Harwich in 1881 by the Norman brothers. These builders were chapel men and, according to the son of one of the Harwich shipwrights, they always gave their craft nonconformist names.

By the 1970s, the Old Gaffers Races had completely altered the sailing fraternity's attitude to the gaff rig. No longer were they considered simply as old craft to be patched up for a few more years' sailing, but owners began to take real pride in their appearance and in the way they sailed them. The East Coast race had by now split up into two separate kinds of entrants; the vast majority who came along for a good day's sail in picturesque company, and the few who turned up determined to win. The main Old Gaffers Trophy usually goes to one of the smaller day racers dating from the Edwardian era, such as the Clyde-built *Golden Plover* which won in 1972, 1973, 1974 and 1978. The *Mayhi* was victorious in 1975 and 1976, and then in 1977 sailmaker Gayle Heard's *Jade* won for the first time and went on to win again in 1979, 1980, 1981, 1982, 1984 and 1985. This 25-foot sloop was built in 1907 on the south coast as one of the Seaview Mermaid Class. (The whole class was later sold to become the Medway One-Design and taken up to the east coast by train.)

Although *Jade* has done well for virtually a decade, her skipper Gayle Heard can never relax because competition is very tough. Jon Wainwright's Mersey River Class *Deva* won the Old Gaffers Trophy in 1971 and consistently does well. The 28-foot *Sheena* won this trophy in 1983, but these noted flyers were challenged by a newcomer in the 1985 race. The first boat home was Peter Brookes's *Asti V*, built as a 6-metre with bermudan rig in 1930 and converted to gaff to take part in this and other local gaff races. She managed to beat Arthur Keeble's East Coast One-Design *Chittabob IV*, built in 1913, but did not win on corrected time. The races are now so popular that people are converting boats to gaff or gunter just to take part, a far cry from the early days when gaff was considered outdated.

Such a variety of craft compete in the Old Gaffers Race today that it has tended to become a series of simultaneous races between different types. None of these 'internal' races is more closely fought than that between former Essex fishing boats. In 1968 it was won for the first time by the 44-foot Brightlingsea smack *ADC*, and she has so far won the trophy more times than any other of the local fishing boats. This beautiful spratting smack was built in about 1890 but was later cut down to a power craft and finished fishing in 1967. As a worn-out fishing craft she could have been abandoned in some lonely creek and left to rot away, but Dick Harman restored her back to sail and helmed her during her era of east coast racing victories.

The *Hyacinth*, a West Mersea oyster dredging smack, was usually hard on the *ADC*'s heels and won the fishing boat trophy in 1972, 1977 and 1978, but this pair's domination of the top places ended in 1982 when the bawley *Helen & Violet* appeared for the first time under a massive topsail, seized victory from them and has carried on winning in the years since. This bawley, another restored fishing boat, carries two suits of sails, one of man-made fibre for racing and the other of traditional material. Racing is only part of the restoration plan; it is seen as equally important that the vessel is actually taken out and used for fishing under sail, as she is not fitted with an engine. Originally such craft had copper boilers for boiling shrimps, which gave them their name.

When the BBC asked to film the 1985 East Coast Old Gaffers Race for the *Under Sail* programme, the two boats selected to take camera crews were the 36-foot bawley *Helen & Violet* and the 49½-foot smack *Sunbeam* – not only because both were large enough for this purpose but also because they were the vessels most likely to win the fishing boat trophy. They represent the best of the Essex coast's traditional small craft. Both types were used for similar kinds of fishing, but in the villages around the Rivers Colne and Blackwater there was a long tradition of the men going away in the summer as paid hands on yachts. The smacks from here therefore evolved hulls similar to those of Victorian yachts, while the bawleys from Harwich, Leigh and Southend were constructed in barge-building yards and actually handle like small spritsail barges because their loose-footed mainsails are inboard of the transom.

In the old days the two types never raced together and the smacks were regarded as by far the faster, so it came as a surprise when the bawley *Helen & Violet* started her recent highly successful racing career. Much of this success is due to the vessel's skipper and part-owner, Jim Lawrence. Jim was brought up in Colchester and left school at fourteen to go away on the sailing barges in the 1950s. He was skipper of the barge *Memory*, trading between London and the east coast ports, mainly in grain. When sailing barges finally had to give way to power vessels, Jim took jobs ashore but was drawn back to skipper the sailing barge *Marjorie* in the new trade of carrying passengers on sailing holidays. This was only summer work, so he started making sails in the winter and finally took the plunge and rented space in Brightlingsea to become a full-time sailmaker.

In 1976, when Jim Lawrence found the *Helen & Violet*, she was at the end of a long hard career as a fishing boat. She had been built by Cann, the barge and bawley builder, at the Gas House Creek yard, Harwich. No trace of Cann's yard remains now, but when the *Helen & Violet* was launched in 1906, Cann was regarded as the best wooden work-boat builder on the coast. The *Helen & Violet* began fishing from Leigh-on-Sea under skipper Sidney Cotgrove, but remained under sail only until the first engine, a 15hp Kelvin, was fitted in 1927. Gradually the sail area was cut down and the engine horsepower increased, and she finally ended up as a full-powered craft fishing out of Tollesbury.

While Jim Lawrence, Cyril White and John Walsh were rebuilding

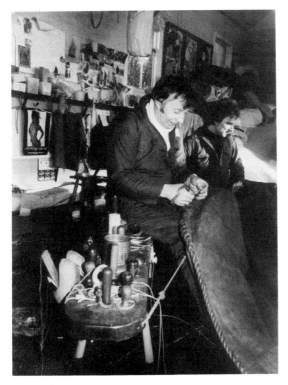

Left: Jim Lawrence,
sailmaker and skipper of the
Helen & Violet

and rigging out the *Helen & Violet* at the dock in Brightlingsea reserved for restored local craft, the hull of *Sunbeam* also lay nearby. All the Essex smacks are fine-lined, but the *Sunbeam* is especially shapely under water. Along with *Neva* and *Xanthe* she must have been built to win races.

While other famous Victorian racing smacks have long since rotted away, the *Sunbeam* survived and with her a reputation as the fastest smack still afloat. However, half a century had passed since she was able to show her paces under sail. When John Rigby bought the *Sunbeam*'s hull, everyone knew that smack racing on the east coast was about to have a thoroughbred in its ranks. The vessel was rebuilt at John Millgate's Peldon yard at the head of Ray Channel. It was Johnnie who had first taken John Rigby out for a sail on his smack *Peace* and lit his enthusiasm for these nimble Essex craft.

The first smack John Rigby restored was the *Charlotte Ellen* in 1977, and he based her at Tollesbury. This Essex village at the head of a muddy creek has in recent years taken a great deal of pride in (and made quite a lot of noise about) the success of the Tollesbury gaff boats in

95

local races. Although John Rigby has done much to encourage the village's traditional boat sailing, he remains a modest man, restoring and sailing smacks because he loves them. Jim Lawrence, skipper of the rival *Helen & Violet*, also has a passion for these traditional work boats, but he is a thoroughly cool professional. His skills come from years of working the sailing barges for a living in all seasons.

The East Coast Old Gaffers Race has always been held in July and, looking back over the years (I am the only person to have entered every race), I can remember many calms with long drifting matches, but there were exceptions – such as in 1966 when the race was sailed in a half-gale. I clearly remember seeing the smack *Pembeth* plough into the tiny *Fanny* in the start off Osea Island, nearly turning her over. Then in 1970 we actually sailed the race in a gale. Only five vessels got round the course, and on my recently bought 34-foot *L'Atalanta* we blew out some of her ancient sails before retiring, none too gracefully, to the shelter of Brightlingsea.

In 1985 a series of gales swept across northern Europe towards the end of July and the East Coast Old Gaffers Race on the 27th was held during a brief blustery gap. The strong winds prevented many boats from even reaching the start and some that did battle on arrived with their crews too exhausted to face another day of hard sailing. Instead of

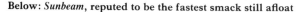

Below: *Sunbeam,* **reputed to be the fastest smack still afloat**

around eighty of the larger Class I and II gaffers starting the race in the River Blackwater off the Stone Sailing Club, only thirty-six, mostly the hardened regulars, manoeuvred for the best starting positions.

Once the starting signal sounded, the fleet turned and roared off before the south-west wind, the speed of the vessels churning the river into a mass of white water. The start happened so quickly that it was difficult to see who was first away, but possibly it was Dick Norris's Whitstable smack *Stormy Petrel*. However, Dick had reefed down (reduced sail) to avoid breakages and this hampered her racing chances.

In the strong squalls some damage did start to appear. The Boston smack *Telegraph* retired after the strain on her mast tore a back stay fitting out of the deck. The Essex smack *Charlotte Ellen* snapped her topmast but carried on with tangled rigging aloft.

The *Sunbeam* and *Helen & Violet* both reefed sail and 'housed' their topmasts (that is, they lowered the top half of their two-part masts), thus reducing the windage aloft and so increasing speed. After some 6 miles, *Sunbeam* was about 200 yards ahead of the *Helen & Violet*. Both craft were creaming along under straining sails and pushing out wide white wakes.

The course for the race, about 24 miles long, goes down the River Blackwater, out to sea and round a triangle made up of channel navigation buoys, and back up the river to the Stone Sailing Club. The entrants actually sail more than 24 miles because, when beating against the wind, they sail a zig-zag course. It was during these beats to windward, the most skilful part of sailing, that the *Helen & Violet* managed to get ahead of the *Sunbeam* and make the North Buxey turning buoy first. After this she went on to complete the triangle and then beat for some 10 miles back to the finish.

The last of the ebb tide was running against the leaders as they beat back up the mile-wide estuary. Four of the smacks went in close to Mersea Island to miss the last of the ebb, as it does not run quite so hard there. With the fleet spread out it was difficult to know quite who was in the lead. The *Charlotte Ellen* was doing well under her new Tollesbury owners and so too was Jack Waterhouse's little King's Lynn smack *Mermaid*.

Back in the river, the *Sunbeam* was rapidly closing the gap with *Helen & Violet* and both were sailing hard in the strong breeze. Then John Rigby's *Sunbeam* made a fatal error and ran ashore near the post marking the entrance to Bradwell Creek. It was not a maritime disaster – the soft grey mud gently brought the great smack to a standstill, where

Above (left to right): *Charlotte Ellen*, *ADC*, *Peace*, *Saxonia*, *Helen & Violet*

she stayed until the rising flood tide floated her again – but it was enough to put her out of the serious racing. *Sunbeam* was eventually the twenty-fourth boat to finish which, on corrected handicap time, made her thirty-fifth out of thirty-six in Classes I and II.

In the remaining few miles to the finish even Jim Lawrence had to put his cup of tea down and devote both hands and full attention to helming the powerful bawley. In front of him were the 'super-gaffers', as the race secretary, Jon Wainwright, calls the open racers. These finished in the following order: 34½-foot *Asti*, 30-foot *Chittabob IV*, 28-foot *Sheena* and the smallest of this group, the 25-foot *Jade*, which on corrected handicap time won the coveted Old Gaffers Trophy. The trophy was presented later at the Stone Sailing Club to *Jade*'s skipper-owner and expert helmsman, the Tollesbury sailmaker Gayle Heard, by his seventy-nine-year-old father, Ted Heard. Ted was in the professional crew of J-class yachts and his father, Edward, was master of J-class yachts.

After the 'super-gaffers', the fishing boats also had a fierce battle in the last frantic beat up from Bradwell to the finish at Stone. The

Mermaid managed to pass the *Charlotte Ellen* and even looked like challenging *Helen & Violet*. Jim and his crew worked like demons, and even in this strong breeze rehoisted the topmast and set a small topsail. The powerful bawley responded by pushing up a wall of white water under her bow and going that little bit faster. She won the fishing-boat prize, but only just, as the *Mermaid* crossed the line a mere 43 seconds after *Helen & Violet* and had cut it so fine that she ran ashore. Hard on her heels, also in a matter of seconds, came the smacks *Charlotte Ellen, Peace* and *ADC* and then, in her best-ever performance, the 34-foot Morecambe Bay prawner *Bonita*, built in 1888 by Crossfield of Arnside who were renowned for building fast fishing boats.

Although there is tough competitive racing among the fast smacks and 'super-gaffers', for many contenders it is the fun of taking part that counts. This is reflected in the rule that no boat is allowed to win more than one of the race prizes, which makes the trophies more evenly distributed over the whole fleet, and in the fact that the Old Gaffers Race has some prizes that are not found in other racing circles. For example, there is a Cup for Trying, given to the boat whose speed (or lack of it) has meant never winning a prize but which has still loyally taken part over a number of years. In 1985 it was presented to *Caliph*, a zulu skiff (Scottish fishing boat) built in about 1900 and setting a dipping lug sail. This complex rig, which requires the sail to be lowered and rehoisted on the opposite side of the mast when beating against the wind, was once extinct but has now been revived. Historically the lug sail descended from the simple squaresail, while the gaff, which is the development of the spritsail, belonged to a different family. The two have united under the flag of the Old Gaffers Association.

Another unusual trophy presented in the East Coast Old Gaffers Race is the Titheridge Trophy, for the first boat home sailed by a man-and-wife crew. This year it went to the Cornish shrimper *Samphire*, one of the new fibreglass-hulled gaffers.

One of the leaders in popularising ferro-cement hulls in Maldon was Austin Edge and after his death his friends gave a trophy in his name for the first ferro-cement-hulled boat in the race. In 1985 it was won by the *Gjoa* which finished eleventh, while the 28-foot ferro-cement *Scalloway* won the Stone Trophy for Class I and II boats under fifty years old, finishing nineteenth. Later that year the *Scalloway* crossed the Atlantic to the West Indies, but planned to be back for the 1986 race.

The *Gjoa* is the fifth boat to be built in the Skua Class. These craft are Colin Archer types (pointed at bow and stern), following the inspiration of the sailing lifeboats designed by the Norwegian Colin Archer in the late nineteenth century. The original 33-foot ferro-cement *Skua* was built in 1977. She too was in the 1985 race, still owned by her builder, Mic Wilkins. His enthusiasm for ferro-cement led Mike Peyton to dub him 'Mic the Brick'. The *Skua* won the Seamanship Cup for completing the course in the stiff breeze after breaking her main boom, temporarily repaired to keep sailing. Although the *Skua* is sailed all the year round, she is now heavy and low in the water with all the Wilkins' worldly possessions aboard, including a coal-burning stove.

The Colin Archers are well suited to strong winds, but for years the owners of Class IV boats – that is, craft over 50-feet long – have been saying that they needed a good breeze to make a good race. This year there was plenty of wind but only the 44-ton ketch *Rainbow Gypsy*, an ex-Grimsby fishing boat (GY 212), came – and she retired. The others went on the Tall Ships Race from Chatham and had a vile time in the North Sea.

At the other end of the scale are the Class IIIs, very small open boats not suitable for going out to sea. In 1985 they sailed a short course just in the River Blackwater, but in the heavy weather it was a very hard race for them, especially in the squalls when they tended to ship a lot of water. Many of the Class III boats were brought in by road, two from the south coast and one, the *Marsh Hare*, from as far away as Cumbria. In all, fourteen boats braved the elements and on the first leg they had to beat hard against wind and tide up to Osea Island. Conditions were too much for some of these brave gaffers: the *Bashful* retired full of water and the Cumbrian *Marsh Hare*, unused to tidal conditions, also had to pull out.

It was the local boats with special knowledge of how to avoid or make use of tidal conditions that won the honours. The West Mersea-based *Native* finished first and was the winner on corrected time. Second place was taken by *Boy Martin* and third was Fabian Bush's *Blackwater Canoe*. The latter vessel was very much in home waters since Fabian Bush is a boatbuilder living on Osea Island, specialising with Jamie Clay in building small wooden craft based on traditional designs. These are just two of the growing number of shipwrights who are reviving wooden boat building on the east coast.

The East Coast Race embraces gaff boats of every type and size and is usually the largest event of its kind in Britain. The Old Gaffers Association has steadily been expanding into other areas. In 1973 races were started on the Clyde and at Dartmouth, and then in 1980 David Cade began the Brighton Old Gaffers Race and Harry Aitken the Falmouth Race. Races have also been started in Sydney and Western Australia, and in Vancouver.

The greatest reward, of course, is the increase in the number of newly built and rebuilt boats appearing. Every summer sees a crop of new gaffers and many members feel that because of this changing state of affairs the Association should be renamed the Gaff Sail Association – dropping the 'old'. However, the word 'gaffer', itself meaning a yacht setting a gaff sail, has firmly entered the English language. The gaff boat owners may have started off battling against the tide in yachting fashions, but now part of the tide has turned to flow with them.

6
ONE-DESIGN YACHT RACING

Jack H. Coote

When one-design and restricted classes were first listed in the 1927 edition of Lloyd's Register of Yachts, there were sixty of them. In 1980, when the latest edition of the Register was published, it included a list of some 250 classes.

While there are significant differences between a strictly controlled one-design class and a restricted class, they do have one very important thing in common – the first boat home in a race is the winner, and it is this fact, more than any other, that explains why so many people choose to race on level terms in yachts which are basically the same. As one owner put it, 'You're not racing money. You're not racing development. It's just man against man and boat against boat.'

When athletes, horses or greyhounds race, to finish first is to win. Fast horses can be slowed by being made to carry extra weight, but the performance of yachts of different types can only be 'equalised' by the application of some form of time allowance, so that the competitors never really know who has won a race until all the boats have finished. This kind of racing, where a calculator is needed to determine how you stand whenever you pass or are passed by another competitor, has little appeal to many sailors and none at all to the spectators on the clubhouse verandah.

Throughout the nineteenth century, yachting was considered the sport of rich men. Their attitude was reflected in a motto attributed to the Royal Yacht Squadron around that time: 'Nothing less than 30-T must ever race with *our* Burgee.' The '30-T' referred to a system of tonnage measurement (TM) devised by the Yacht Racing Association in 1881, the formula for which was:

$$\frac{(\text{Waterline length} + \text{Beam})^2 \times \text{Beam}}{1730} = \text{Tonnage}$$

Thus the 30-T minimum of the RYS would have related to a yacht of some 40 or 50 feet.

The YRA 'tonnage' formula proved ill-suited to the rating of racing yachts because it led to their being designed to 'cheat' the rule by having extremely narrow beam, excessive draught and tremendous sail areas. The worst example of this 'plank-on-edge' type was the *Oona*, with her waterline length of 34 feet, a beam of 5½ feet and a draught of 8 feet! The *Oona* was wrecked while on her delivery passage from Wivenhoe in Essex to Belfast in 1886, and her designer was lost.

The next measurement rule was proposed by the famous yacht designer Dixon Kemp, who took into consideration both waterline length and sail area, using this formula:

$$\frac{\text{Waterline length} \times \text{Sail area}}{6000} = \text{Rating}$$

Division by 6000 resulted in a 40-tonner having a rating of about 40, while a 20-tonner came out at around a 20-rating. This went some way towards facilitating the change-over from the earlier system of measurement.

The Dixon Kemp rating rule proved reasonably successful at first, so that by 1893 yachts were racing as 40-raters, 20-raters, 5-raters, 2½-raters and even ½-raters, a few of which may still be seen sailing on the Thames at Surbiton. Before long, however, designers had again found a way round the rule – this time by building yachts with over-hanging bows and sterns, increasing their effective waterline so that they would go faster when heeled. This form of rule 'cheating' resulted in 'skimming dishes' with overhangs amounting to almost as much again as waterline length, together with great beam and a fin keel with a bulb of lead. So once again, only by commissioning a new yacht every year could anyone be sure of staying ahead of the fleet.

The dissatisfaction that would result was foreseen by Major Heckstall-Smith in his book *The Complete Yachtsman* when he wrote: 'A serious trouble developed in 1896 in the smaller classes. This was the rapidity with which new boats outclassed the older ones. In the "little raters" a boat scarcely lasts a season before it is outclassed.'

This high cost of obsolescence was not the only reason why yacht racing remained the exclusive sport of rich men until almost the end of the last century. At that time no owner skippered his own yacht and certainly would have nothing whatever to do with its maintenance, so there were considerable additional expenses and, as the *Badminton Library* states: 'The owner of a 5-rater can consider himself fortunate if he can secure the services of a good man as skipper for 30s a week, clothes (about 5s worth), 20s racing money for a first prize and 10s for a second or third prize.' In addition, 'it would cost from £100 to £150 [about £4500 today] to maintain and race a 5- or 2½-rater for twenty weeks of the season. This sum covers a crew of two paid hands, and the owner of a 5 must enlist two or three Corinthians to help at each race.' The dictionary definition of a Corinthian is a 'man of fashion or pleasure', which gives some idea of the style in which yachts were raced in those days.

At about this time, new yacht clubs were appearing round the coast of Great Britain, with very different aims from those of the Royal Yacht Squadron of the YRA. The members of these new clubs simply wanted to sail and race their own boats at a moderate cost, an attitude reflected in the reasons given for the formation of one of the new groups, the Bembridge Sailing Club. In 1890 the Bembridge men thought that 'a club whose leading feature would be racing in boats of uniform pattern would be a success'. Their idea was to have a fleet of 'club boats, sloop-rigged, with rolling jibs and mainsails so as to reef easily. The subscription to these boats being only £1, a member is enabled to have a summer's sailing and cruising for this small sum, and can, if he is a fair hand in a boat, win good prizes. The boats are as near as possible equal, and lots being drawn for them before racing, the best man wins as a rule.' . . . in other words, one-design racing.

H. C. Folkard, in the sixth edition of his classic book *The Sailing Boat*, published in 1906, devoted a whole section to the one-design classes of those days, of which he wrote:

> The introduction of a one-design class is the result of the uncertainty and dissatisfaction occasioned by the rules of measurement and rating of the Yacht Racing Association as applied to small racing yachts, the frequent alteration of those rules, and the facilities afforded for evasion, whereby unfair advantages have been gained, coupled with the expense attendant on the short career of a racing boat under such rules, involving the building of a new boat nearly every season.

The revolution was also described in humorous terms in *Yachting Monthly* under the title 'The Paid Hand and the ABOD Class':

> And when all the chiefs of the tribes of the Ancient Britons had built unto themselves great boats of wondrous design, they went out and sailed one against the other and the other against the one so long as pots, the receptacles of mead, were offered to those who came in first, and men they took from their tribes and compelled them to work in their boats, and from the soil they took the tillers thereof and placed them in their boats to steer. And these were the days of the Unpaid Hand.
>
> But these men murmured among themselves and said, 'We have left our little rocky caves for you and raced for you so that ye might win many pots, and with nothing have you rewarded us, not even with the wherewithal to buy mead. Therefore will we be slaves no longer.' And the chiefs retired to a safe distance, and,

after many chins had wagged, the chiefs climbed down and said, 'Ye men of the tribes who race, henceforth shall ye be known as Paid Hands, for many gifts shall ye receive for the little work ye do. Free caves shall ye also have to dwell in, new suits of the finest skins shall be given unto you at every sixth moon, and nothing but the best and freshest English ichthyosaurus shall be served unto you for food, for never shall ye eat preserved flesh from distant Jungles. Half our prize-money will we give unto you, and should there be anything else it is for the asking.' And the Paid Hands went back to the yachts and raced.

Thus was the racing of the chiefs a matter of great cost, and only those who had much land could enter into it. And the little men sat on the shore and shook their heads sadly, for they loved the waters, but could not afford to sail thereon. Then one rose and said, 'Lo! my brothers. If many men can sail a big boat, cannot one man sail a small one? Let us each take unto himself a small tree, and build each a boat so that in the length thereof, and the breadth thereof, and the depth thereof all are equal, so that when the boats are finished the other shall be as like unto which as which is like unto the other.' And the little men rejoiced, and the Ancient Britons' One-Design Class flourished exceedingly.

Not only did Heckstall-Smith, who was secretary of YRA between 1897 and 1944, clearly see and write about the advantages of one-design racing. W. P. (later Sir William) Burton, presiding at a dinner of the Orwell Corinthian Yacht Club in 1912, said, 'Those that have given this matter the consideration that the YRA had done knew that it was only by having a one-design class that it was possible to have cheap small boat racing in a satisfactory way.'

As late as 1937 Uffa Fox was pleading with the International Yacht Racing Union to 'foster and encourage one-design class racing' because 'the purpose of such a class is to make all the boats, their rigs and sails, as alike as possible, so that a man wins by his superior skill in sailing and the care he has taken to keep his boat in perfect condition.'

Despite all this evidence that attitudes and requirements had changed, the supporters of one-design racing got little help from the Yacht Racing Association until 1946, when the Council approved their very first true one-design – the 12-foot moulded-ply Firefly dinghy. It is true that in 1919 they had thought about introducing a YRA one-design class of about 16 feet, but the Draft Report of the Rating Rules Committee of that year went no further than to say: 'The design of this class is to be selected'. In the face of this disinterest, local yacht clubs had no alternative but to set about changing things for themselves, introducing their own one-design classes between 1890 and 1914 and again between the two World Wars.

After almost a hundred years it would probably be impossible to compile a completely accurate chronological list of all the early one-design classes. The *Guinness Book of Yachting Facts and Feats* tells us that the world's first one-design class was the Water Wag of Dublin Bay, which started racing in 1887. The early Water Wags were 13-foot open boats with iron centre-plates and an optional gunter rig on a mast limited in height to 13 feet. At one time the fleet numbered twenty boats and it was reported that 'the skill with which they were managed, the closeness of the contests and the excitement and amusement they have afforded from time to time have been appreciated by the throngs of spectators who come to see the sport of the Water Wags.' An important rule of the class stated: 'It is one of the fundamental purposes of the Water Wags that the boats shall be similar in every respect save sail plan.'

In 1888 a Water Wag cost between £15 and £25 complete, 'a silk racing lug from Lapthorn and Ratsey alone coming to £2 15s [£2.75].' There were no plans for the first boat, which was apparently a Norwegian pram with a boiler-plate fitted as a centre-board; but full-size tracings of the builder's moulds could be obtained by 'sending 2s to the Society for Employment of Women, 21 Kildare Street, Dublin'. Several other one-design classes were established in Ireland around the same time; for example, the Fife-designed Belfast Lough ODs in 1897 and the Mylne-designed Star Class ODs in 1900.

Then in 1902 thirteen 22-foot boats, known as the Belfast Fairies, were built for £50 each to a design by Linton Hope. That the Fairies gave good sport can be gathered from the enthusiastic comments of one of their skippers:

> If one-design racing resolves itself into beating to windward, Mr Linton Hope gave us boats which are a treat to steer on the wind, especially with a little bit of sea on. The powerful quarters and sharp waterlines forward make these 'Fairies' most weatherly craft. They have only 15 cwt of iron on the keel, and are wonderfully 'corky'. Some people might call them unduly tender, but once they get their deck down to the water they stay there, and heeling over helps to keep the crew dry.

They must have been pretty well built, too, since some of them were still racing fifty years later.

It was also in 1902 that John Wylie designed the Waverley Class, an 18-foot keel boat, for members of the County Antrim Yacht Club. Much later, in 1936, the rules of the class were modified to permit the use of the new-fangled 'gaff-less' rig, but those who tried it all eventually reverted to the original gunter rig. The Waverley Class very nearly died in 1949, after one of the boats foundered on passage from Bangor to Whitehead; but by 1960, four had found their way to the

Ballyholme Yacht Club and since then the class has regained strength until now, over eighty years after it was started, about a dozen Waverleys are again racing in Belfast Lough.

The Seabird, a 20-foot carvel-built, gunter-rigged, ballasted centreboard sloop, was designed jointly by Herbert Baggs and Scott Hayward of Belfast in 1898, and would have measured as a ½-rater except that the boats were almost always raced as a one-design class. They were to cost no more than £35 complete and were in fact built for £34 17s 6d (£34.87½)! As with so many of the ODs that followed, the sail area of the Seabird was limited to 200 square feet, although a small spinnaker was allowed even in those days. The club that commissioned the design was the West Lancashire Yacht Club of Southport, but it was not long before a second fleet was established by the Donaghadee Sailing Club on Belfast Lough, although they called their boats the Seashells and named them accordingly. A third club, the Gourock Yacht Club, adopted the class on the Clyde and named their boats the Gaels, while a fourth fleet, called the Cariads, was established at Caernarvon.

In 1910 Donaghadee Sailing Club wanted to sell its eleven Seashells. The committee of the West Kirby Sailing Club bought the lot and then sold them to members on a 'first come, first served' basis, provided the names of the boats were changed from seashells to seabirds. By this time a Seabird Class Association had been formed and that its rules were strictly enforced can be seen from the way the Association dealt with a problem in 1912. It seems that a man named Roberts of Chester had been given authority to build five Seabirds for members of the West Kirby club, but took it upon himself to build six. He then sought permission from the club to sell the extra boat as a genuine Seabird – which it undoubtedly was. But the club refused to grant him authority and it was not until fifty years later, in 1963, that they relented and Seabird sail No. 33 was allocated to that boat under the name *Sea Snipe*.

Although known as the West Kirby Star Class for well over sixty years, this class was actually begun by the West Lancashire Yacht Club in 1907 when the club introduced 'a new inexpensive class of boat – intended for use by the younger and less experienced club members.' To ensure that this purpose was met, one of the class rules prohibited 'any past or present helmsman of any local class from steering a Star Class boat in any West Lancs race.'

West Lancashire Yacht Club sailed and raced their Stars until 1922, when they sold the fleet of five boats to the West Kirby Sailing Club which, twelve years earlier, had bought all its Seabirds from Donaghadee Sailing Club. A ballot was held to decide which of the West Kirby members could buy a Star and each purchaser had to agree not to offer his boat for sale outside the club. From time to time since then new Stars have been built, two of them as recently as 1981 – when the cost was over £4000 compared with the original price of £32!

The Star is a tough, clinker-built, half-decked boat with an overall length of 16 feet 9 inches and a draught of only 1½ feet with the iron plate up. Additional stability comes from 5 cwt of inside ballast so that 160 square feet of sail can be carried. Both main and jib are red and the gunter mainsail bears a large white star with the boat's number imprinted within it.

Below: *Mercury*, a West Kirby Star Class One-Design

The West Kirby Sailing Club had resulted from a breakaway group leaving the older Hoylake club, formed in 1887. By 1902 the Hoylake Sailing Club was already racing its one-design boats: the famous Hoylake Opera Class. The Operas may not look very impressive, but they have given good sport to members of that club since the dawn of the century, so there cannot be much wrong with them.

Designed by a man named Latta who may have been influenced by the Dublin Water Wags, the original moulds were kept and have been used to build younger boats. The clinker-built hull of an Opera is 16 feet overall and only 6 inches less on the waterline, and it draws just 1 foot with the centre-plate up – a necessary feature of the shallow entrance at Hoylake. The rig, which is particularly interesting, has remained the same despite experiments with a bermuda sail. The main is a high peaked lugsail with a loose foot, and although the jib is necessarily small because of a short mast, frequent use is made of a spinnaker.

In 1893, a meeting of the committee of the Solent Sailing Club reported that it 'viewed with the greatest concern the ever-increasing expenditure attendant on small-class racing in the Solent. It is strongly of the opinion that the sport should be conducted in a manner suitable to the means of the majority, and not merely with a view to the encouragement of the few who can afford year after year to build a new boat.' The outcome was the formation of the first one-design fleet in the Solent, appropriately named the Solent One-Design Class and based on a design by H. W. White whose company, White Brothers, built the boats at Itchen Ferry.

By comparison with the Redwings and the 'X' One-Designs that came later, the Solent OD was really a yacht, being 33 feet overall and carrying 750 square feet of sail. Nevertheless, by 1899 the class had grown to some twenty craft and it became necessary to race in two divisions for two sets of prizes.

In the autumn of 1896 some members of the Royal Victoria Yacht Club of Ryde and the Bembridge Sailing Club met together with the object of 'starting a small class of boats for amateur racing, the ½-raters having become too expensive and too soon outclassed for many to care to build. It was decided to introduce a small racing boat which would not be too large for single-handed racing, to rely entirely on amateurs as crew and to abolish the paid hand.' The Redwing Club was then formed and the famous J-class designer C. E. Nicholson was commissioned to prepare a design. The result was the original 22-foot Solent Redwing.

From the outset the Redwings were never a true one-design class, for

while their hulls were made as nearly alike as possible, their rig was left entirely optional, provided that it did not exceed 200 square feet of sail. This rule really meant what it said – even the extra area resulting from a curved leech is measured and included. In the early days of the class, before the merits of the bermudan rig were fully appreciated, Redwing owners experimented enthusiastically with balanced lugsails and lateen sails, as well as a variety of gaff and gunter rigs. Whatever the chosen rig, the colour of the sailcloth was always the distinctive red by which the class is so easily recognised.

In 1938, some forty years after the first fourteen boats had been built, the Redwing Club decided to replace the class with a new design, once again by Charles Nicholson. The 'new' Redwing is 28 feet overall and has a waterline length of 20 feet. It is a keel boat that retains the shallow draught often required to leave and enter Bembridge harbour as well as the freedom to 'do as you like' with 200 square feet of sail. While most owners of the new boats used the bermuda rig, two (including Lord Brabazon of aircraft fame) tried out the Lungstrom rig with its boomless sail and unstayed mast. This unusual sail proved effective to windward, but the limit to sail area precluded the opportunity to 'goose-wing' down-wind, so there are no Lungstrom-rigged Redwings today. Freedom of choice as to rig no doubt explains some of the success of the first generation of Redwings, but the continuing popularity of the present class must be due to their sound design and good looks.

As previously noted, in 1890 the Bembridge Sailing Club had decided to build a number of club boats of 'uniform design'. These 16-foot square-stemmed, transom-sterned craft were not very attractive and were in any case intended for use only by beginners. But they did incorporate one novel feature – a combined mainsail and topsail devised by Captain Du Boulay, which came to be known as the 'Bembridge sail'.

In 1904 a much more attractive one-design class resulted from the joint ideas of a member of the club, E. C. Cockburn, and Alfred Westmacott, who was subsequently responsible for so many one-design boats. This Bembridge OD was just over 20 feet long with a waterline length of 15½ feet, a beam of 5 feet 10 inches and a draught of 3 feet. The boats were clinker built, had an iron keel as well as a centre-plate, and they set 200 square feet of sail with a gaff main and a roller foresail. The centre-plates were removed at some time during the history of the class, which must have been very successful, since sixty such boats had been built by 1912.

Opposite: *Geisha*, one of the Hoylake Opera Class ODs

In 1933 the old 1904 Bembridge ODs were replaced by a new design – again by Westmacott. The new boats were built by Woodnutt of St Helens, but this time they were of carvel construction.

In 1934 a local newspaper reported that more than 200 small craft were kept in Portsmouth Harbour and that 'where vigorous racing did exist, it came in the one-design classes, where a good number of competitors started and raced together on level terms. The Portchester Ducks Class is a fine example and some half-dozen former Bembridge one-design class boats race regularly in the harbour.' It was in this climate that a group of local yachtsmen formed the Portsmouth Harbour Racing and Sailing Association and decided to establish 'a harbour one-design' to be called the Victory Class. They were probably influenced by the half-dozen boats already racing in the harbour since 'the ex-Bembridge Sailing Club One-Design came to mind'.

The original drawings of the 1904 Bembridge One-Design had been lost. Lines were therefore taken off one of the old boats and new templates and a keel mould were made – first for use by Harry Feltham of Portsmouth and later by Hamper of Fareham. All the new boats were given a bermudan rig designed by Charles Nicholson, and although some of the old boats remained gaff-rigged for a while, they too were eventually converted to the more modern sail plan.

The Victory Class is distinctive in several ways. The sail insignia is a 'Z' and all the clinker-built hulls are painted black with a boot-topping colour to indicate the club of the owner: green for the Royal Albert Yacht Club, scarlet for the Portsmouth Sailing Club, white for Royal Navy Sailing Association and sky-blue for the Royal Air Force Sailing Club. Victory Class boats race for some eighteen trophies each season and it is quite usual for the number of entries to exceed twenty – not bad for a hull design that dates back to 1904.

The largest one-design keel boat class in the Solent is the 'X' Class One-Design, originally sponsored by the Motor Yacht Club in 1909 when that establishment was based at Netley on Southampton Water. An 'X' boat can be built by one or other of only two builders – Burnes of Bosham or Clare Lallow of Cowes. The design was once again the work of Alfred Westmacott, and the hull has an overall length of 20 feet 8⅜ inches, an indication of the precision with which the class is controlled, as is the rule which determines that the seams of the hull 'must be caulked with cotton and stopped; splines or close seams are not allowed'. One of the few freedoms the owner of an 'X' boat has is to choose the length of his tiller, which in any case 'must be of wood'.

Above: Four of the ninety 'X' Class ODs which raced in very strong winds on the Solent during Cowes Week 1985

There are 'X' Class divisions at Cowes, Hamble, Itchenor, Lymington, Parkstone and Yarmouth, and over the years some 180 'X' boats have been built of which about 150 are still sailing. The weather was extremely boisterous during Cowes Week in 1985, yet no less than ninety 'X' ODs competed. The original gaff rig was compulsory until 1928 and remained optional until 1950, but by 1933 most of the fleet had adopted the 'new' rig, although metal spars are still not permitted.

The Seaview Mermaids were preceded by the Ark One-Design Class, although not much is known about them except that they were 16 feet overall, clinker-built, gaff-rigged and had a straight stem with a bowsprit. There were about eight Arks sailing at Seaview between 1902 and 1907, when the Mermaid Class first made its appearance. The first-generation Mermaids were much more shapely boats than the

Arks, being three-quarter-decked with a counter stern and a short bowsprit. As Robert Simper records, the whole of the first Mermaid fleet was sold to the Medway Yacht Club in the 1920s to become the Medway One-Design Class, and in recent years *Jade*, one of the original 1907 boats, has regularly won the Old Gaffers Trophy on the east coast.

The second generation of Mermaids, the type that is still sailing from Seaview, were designed by Westmacott and built by Woodnutt in the spring and summer of 1922. The 'new' boats were about the same size as their predecessors, but from the outset they were bermudan-rigged. In 1948, when the Seaview Yacht Club owned ten Mermaids as club boats, an interesting system of grading the helmsmen who would sail them was introduced:

> Grade 'A' helmsmen were expected to be able to handle a boat in a seamanlike manner in any weather considered fit for racing, and to have full knowledge of the Rules. Grade 'B' helmsmen were permitted to sail at any time with a Grade 'A' sailor in the boat and could take boats themselves in fair weather with the consent of the Race Officer.
>
> Ungraded helmsmen were only permitted to sail when accompanied by a Grade 'A' helmsman, who became responsible for the boat.

It is said that during Cowes Week of 1922 the 'new' Mermaid attracted such favourable attention that members of the Hamble River Sailing Club asked Alfred Westmacott to design them an 'improved' Mermaid, with which to form the Sunbeam Class. Although their waterline lengths are practically the same, the overhangs of a Sunbeam make it some 2 feet longer than the Mermaid and 6 feet longer overall than the 'X' boat. Woodnutt built thirty-nine Sunbeams between 1922 and 1938, first at St Helens on the Isle of Wight and later at Warsash, where the already-mentioned fire brought an end to the company and the loss of the original Sunbeam plans. The Sunbeam Class was first formed at Hamble and remained there until 1930, when the base was transferred to Bembridge. At this time the fleet numbered twenty-four – the maximum permitted under a class rule. This meant that when two more boats were built for owners at Itchenor, they were debarred from racing with the class. However, after the Second World War the tables were turned when the restriction on numbers was removed and the class headquarters moved to Itchenor.

A Falmouth Sunbeam Division was formed by the Royal Cornwall Yacht Club in 1924 and in recent years there have sometimes been more Sunbeams at Falmouth than in Chichester Harbour. Sunbeams have raced during every Cowes Week since 1923.

It is not widely known, even on the east coast, that the Royal Corinthian Yacht Club began in 1872 as the Corinthian Yacht Club and resulted from a letter to the Editor of *The Field* in which the writer expressed the opinion that 'a club might be formed for vessels under 15 tons with a convenient rendezvous such as Erith'. Soon after the letter appeared, a meeting and a dinner were held at the Pier Hotel, Erith, and in November of that year the first general meeting of the Corinthian Yacht Club took place at the Cannon Street Hotel, where it was announced that there were already '249 members with 74 vessels'. At that same momentous meeting a new rating rule was announced that would bring draught into the measurement of yachts for racing purposes. This was radical thinking, because at that time yachts were still being designed to the Tonnage Measurement Rule mentioned earlier, thus penalising their beam but not their draught.

In 1879 the first Corinthian clubhouse was opened at Erith and in 1892 the club received the 'Royal' title, while in that same year a branch was opened in a room in the White Hart Hotel at Burnham-on-Crouch. The following year saw the London Sailing Club of Hammersmith also start a branch at Burnham, and at the end of that season a joint regatta was held – the forerunner of Burnham Week.

In 1895 the Royal Corinthian Yacht Club introduced the Dabchick One-Design, a 20-foot keel boat designed by Linton Hope, who specified a fully battened bermudan mainsail. Although twenty of them were built, these innovative craft proved to be easily capsized even after the rig had been changed to lugsail and lead keels had been fitted.

By 1901 the Royal Corinthian Yacht Club had moved its headquarters to Port Victoria on the Isle of Grain, where the oil refinery is today. This must have been a prosperous period for the club, since during the previous year it had also built a clubhouse on Prior's Wharf at Burnham. There were doubts about the wisdom of moving to Port Victoria and a somewhat confusing period seems to have followed, during which a 'new' 30-foot Corinthian One-Design, by G. U. Laws of Burnham, was introduced at Port Victoria, while a 22-foot Seabird OD class by Pain Clark was adopted at Burnham. This Seabird design was unrelated to the quite different boats controlled by the Seabird Association.

During the winter of 1913–14 it was apparently decided to change the name of the 30-foot Corinthian One-Design Class to the East Coast OD, and in the summer of 1914 five boats were still racing at Burnham and four at Port Victoria, although all of them had been built in King's yard on the Crouch.

During the First World War three of the Medway ECODs were at the bottom of the river for a time, and for a few years after the War the class went through a very thin time. There were about six boats racing at Burnham during the 1920s, but by the following decade the fleet had increased to nine. These were fairly large yachts, at that time often raced with the aid of a paid hand and usually owned by 'established men of substance, who spent money fully on sails and maintenance'. So, when the smaller Royal Corinthian OD was introduced in 1934, it was generally assumed that the older class of larger boats would die, and there was even talk by some members of 'old hulks taking up valuable mooring space'.

After some lean years in the 1950s and 1960s, however, a change in attitude on the part of a new group of youthful, not-so-rich owners brought new life into the class, so that by the early 1970s, sixty years after their introduction, ten ECODs were racing once again. Most of the new generation of owners were under thirty-five and the old boats, now without paid hands, came to be known as a young man's class: in particular the 'young marrieds' class, 'since the girls seemed to love it and only let up to have another baby' – a far cry from the days before 1930, when women were even not allowed into the Royal Corinthian clubhouse.

Sadly, the ECODs no longer race on the Crouch, but many people now know how handsome they look from the appearance of *Joyce* in the *Under Sail* television programme. *Joyce* is now in the care of Paul Kyle, a traditionalist who will no doubt see to it that when the boat reaches her century she is still sailing on the river where she was built.

Chittabob IV, one of the three original 1913 boats, is also still around, having reverted to gaff rig in order to compete regularly in the annual East Coast Old Gaffers Race.

Those who saw the *Under Sail* programme will also know what the present-day Royal Corinthian One-Design looks like. She typifies the small, open-cockpit, day-racing keel boat that has done so much for the sport of sailing around our shores for almost a hundred years. The RCOD was designed by Harry Smith, whose company at Burnham built most of the fleet, although four others were built at King's yard and two more by Stone of Brightlingsea. The first boat, *Coral Nymph*, was afloat by the end of 1934 and by the next season sixteen were racing – but never on Sundays! At least ten RCODs still race regularly on the unpredictable waters of the Crouch estuary.

At first the class had jibs on rollers with jib-booms that could be

Above: RCOD *Corindelle* during Burnham Week 1985

pulled round, square-on when running, because no spinnakers were allowed until after the Second World War when Norman Dallimore was asked to modernise the sail plan. Owners then found that flying a spinnaker put extra strains on the hulls and it became necessary to allow new oak floors, hanging-knees and tie rods to be fitted. Unlike its counterpart, the 'X' One-Design Class in the Solent, the RCOD adopted a metal mast and boom as well as slab-reefing in the 1970s.

Although the Royal Burnham Yacht Club is not quite as old as the Royal Corinthian, its 20-foot one-design preceded the Corinthian

Above: RBOD *Arial* on the River Crouch

equivalent by two or three years. In 1932 the Royal Burnham commissioned Norman Dallimore, the local designer, to draw a 20-foot keel boat with 250 square feet of bermuda-rigged sail. The very satisfactory result was a stiff, beamy hull with plenty of freeboard to ensure good heavy-weather performance. For a time the class was also established by the Colne Yacht club at Brightlingsea, where it was known as the 'Pye Fleet'.

From the time the London–Tilbury–Southend railway line was opened in 1850, more and more people came to live along the north shore of the Thames estuary between Southend and Leigh-on-Sea, and by the turn of the century three yacht clubs were established to the west of the pier: the Alexandra, Westcliff and Essex Yacht Clubs.

By 1912 the Alexandra Yacht Club (the 'Alex') was concerned that the popularity of the 17-foot open-boat class it was sailing at the time had been 'marred by the advent of three new boats ingeniously contrived to evade the restrictions, and these have practically swept the board, so that the older boats have no chance in the racing'. Clearly the time had come to introduce a one-design; but the special conditions imposed by the drying flats off the Southend shore precluded the use of a keel boat and the choice had to be a centre-boarder – and quite a tough one at that.

As usual, a committee was formed, including some members of the Essex Yacht Club, to recommend a one-design suitable for racing over the flats and in the deep and often rough water of the fairway. A design was commissioned from Morgan Giles of Teignmouth, who drew an 18-foot half-decked clinker-built boat with a beam of 6 feet and a draught of 10 inches with its 1½-cwt centre-plate retracted. Up to 2-cwt of moveable lead ballast was also permitted. The sail area was an ample 210 square feet, which at the outset was in the form of a gunter rig on either solid wood or bamboo spars. The Thames Estuary One-Design or TEOD (the 'Tee-od') that resulted became one of the best-known boats in the history of Thames estuary sailing. Anyone who learned to sail in one always reckons that they served a sound apprenticeship. At the end of the new design's first season, one of the skippers described a day's racing:

> You wake up with the windows rattling like fury, get to the Club and listen to the club balcony critics who decide that your boat hasn't got an earthly, and then get into oilies. Going off to the moorings, you get your feet soaked because the dinghy leaks like a sieve, and you get under way. At last the gun goes and a dozen of you go reaching for the pierhead and luffing each other to Gravesend or somewhere up that way. Perhaps you get free, if you have had the pluck to get into what at first looks like a losing position, but soon turns into a winning one when the others have finished their luffing. You fling round the Pier Buoy and with hardened sheets plug to the Low Way, soaked to the skin and with most of the breath knocked out of your body. If your gear has stood it and the boat isn't too full of water, you gybe round the Low Way, and with spinnaker set charge like a runaway horse homewards, yawing about and perhaps having to run by the lee for a while with your boom poking a hole in the sky. Then you make your more dead than alive forrard hand give you a spell and you can have a suck at the pipe and a flask, and prepare for the next round, which will be worse than the first, with the strong ebb running.

The TEOD was a success and was soon adopted by several other clubs, including Leigh-on-Sea Sailing Club, the Nore Yacht Club (now defunct), the Westcliff Yacht Club and the East Lothian Yacht Club on the Forth. In 1919, prompted no doubt by the pre-war enterprise of the club next door and the need to replace their old 17-foot restricted class of open boats, the Essex Yacht Club asked Morgan Giles to go one better and 'improve' his earlier design for the Alexandra Yacht Club. The resulting Essex One-Design had a slightly harder bilge with maximum beam carried further aft, a heavier centre-plate and a more roomy cockpit – 'for family sailing'.

The new boats were all bermuda-rigged, although they need not have been since the type of sail was optional within the limit of 210 square feet. Nine Essex ODs were built initially by Cole and Wiggin at Leigh-on-Sea and the rolled-veneer hollow spars were made by McGruer of Clynder on the Gareloch. The price for the first batch of boats was £100 each! Like the TEODs before them, the EODs were successful and very soon fleets of them were racing at Ramsgate, Margate, Herne Bay, Whitstable and on the Medway. The height of their popularity came around 1950, by which time over seventy boats had been built and twenty-nine raced as a class in that year's Kent

Below: Essex One-Designs rounding the inner Crouch buoy during Burnham Week, with a TEOD (just visible at left) running down to the mark

Yachting Week, when the series was won by 'Buzz' Mountstevens in
Nocturne.

In 1933 the YRA, recognising the success of the Thames estuary
boats, introduced the National 18-foot Restricted Class, together with
the dispensation that existing TEODs and EODs would be entitled to
race on level terms with the new 18-footers.

Several clubs whose members sailed on the rivers and broads of East
Anglia had established their own one-design classes by the early years of
this century. The Orwell Corinthian ODs first raced in the Harwich
Regatta of 1899, when the Royal Harwich Yacht Club was still based at
the Pier Hotel. These boats were designed by H.C. Smith, who thirty
years later designed the Royal Corinthian OD. The Orwell class boats
were 18 feet overall with a beam of 5 feet 3 inches and a draught of 2 feet
10 inches with a fin keel. They were rigged with a gunter mainsail and a
roller jib set on a short bowsprit. No plans ever seem to have been
published, but moulds were still to be found at King's yard at Pin Mill
until the 1950s.

In 1936 Robert Clark was asked by the Royal Harwich Yacht Club to
design a new class to replace the old Orwell ODs, and an initial batch
were built to the new plans at Sittingbourne in Kent. They were
transom-sterned fin-keel boats with the typical one-design length of 20
feet but with a greater than average beam of 6 feet 10 inches. The
permitted sail area was a precise 179 square feet. Unfortunately, the
Second World War limited the growth of this class, although seven
boats are still racing in the Orwell.

During the 1920s and 1930s Robert Stone of Brightlingsea designed
and built several open and half-decked one-design boats for nearby clubs
on the Colne and Blackwater. One of the most popular was the Brightlingsea OD, some of which are still racing in the Colne regattas. Another was
the West Mersea Sprite, of which there were twenty or so by 1939.

The Orford White Wings, so called because of their 'snow-white'
appearance, were introduced on the Rivers Ore and Alde during
1898–9. The design, by Sibbick of Cowes, was for a gaff-rigged yacht,
23 feet overall and 16 feet 8 inches on the waterline, with a beam of 6 feet
and a draught of 3 feet. The 226 square feet of sail was balanced by a
14-cwt keel. The class raced from Orford in the river and also at sea off
Felixstowe and Harwich Harbour. Early enthusiasm for the White
Wings can be gauged by the fact that, during the 1900 season, they
competed in forty-seven match races.

Further up river at Aldeburgh, the Redwing class of 12½-foot dinghies dates back to the early days of the century. They are hardly likely to be confused with the much larger Redwings of the Solent. The little clinker-built Aldeburgh boats, with their turkey-red lugsails, were used as a nursery class at Slaughden Quay during school holidays. The Lapwing OD Class of dinghies that followed in 1947 were designed by Morgan Giles and again were intended mainly for children.

In the mid-1930s some members of the Aldeburgh Yacht Club decided to buy seven of the Gareloch ODs that had been racing on the Clyde since 1924 but had now been ousted by a new fleet of Dragons. The Gareloch OD was designed and built by McGruer of Clynder and is 24 feet overall with a waterline length of 16½ feet and a beam of 5½

Below: Broads One-Designs, also called 'Brown Boats'

feet. The keel, ballasted with 15-cwt of iron, allows a sail area of 250 square feet.

The Broads One-Design Class, formed in 1900, was based on a design by the famous Linton Hope. Although the boats were mainly intended for racing on the protected waters of the Broads, they were quite capable of facing the open sea off Lowestoft, although their 250 square feet of sail may often have been reefed. The 'Brown Boats', as these varnished Broads ODs are affectionately called, are 27-foot carvel-built keel boats, somewhat saucer-like in appearance with a long counter and a waterline length of only 16 feet. After more than eighty years the 'Brown Boats' can still be seen racing at the Broads regattas.

The Yare and Bure 20-foot one-design keel boat was introduced in 1908 and is notable for the 280 square feet of sail it carries. By 1939 this class numbered nearly fifty craft, and more were stationed at the Lowestoft and Oulton Broad Yacht Club where they were known as the Waveney ODs.

In 1898 a goods train arrived in a siding at Bridlington carrying the hulls of eight handsome keel boats that had been built in Southampton by Field & Co. to a design by J.S. Helyer of Itchen Ferry. When rigged, these yachts were to form the original Yorkshire One-Design Class belonging to members of the Royal Yorkshire Yacht Club. The new boats were 25 feet overall with a waterline length of 18 feet, a beam of 6 feet 9 inches and a draught of 3½ feet. They each had an 18-cwt iron keel and 5-cwt of moveable ballast. The sail area was 320 square feet in the form of a gunter main and a roller foresail 'to enable them to regulate the spread of that sail according to circumstances of wind and sea'. The YODs were three-quarter-decked and said to be 'absolutely uncapsizeable'. The class permitted the use of spinnakers, but with the following rather nice proviso: 'If any yacht starts a race single-handed, the other competitors are to be informed of this and in such case no spinnaker or reaching foresail may be used by any competitor.'

In Glasgow, like Liverpool a prosperous city at the turn of the century, there was enough money about for many people to take up the relatively new sport of yacht racing. The Firth of Clyde, easily reached by rail and steamer, offered unequalled waters for both cruising and racing from the two well-established clubs – the Royal Clyde Yacht Club at Hunters Quay on the Holy Loch and the Royal Northern Yacht Club at Rothesay. The flourishing state of yachting in 1900 was summed up at the time by Folkard: 'The pastime as pursued on the Clyde waters could not be in a healthier state than at present, and the demand for boats is such that no craft of merit need wait long to find a purchaser.'

One of the earliest classes on the Clyde was the 23-foot Waterline Restricted Class, designed by the famous G.L. Watson in 1890 for the Royal Clyde Yacht Club. Two years later Watson also designed most of the smaller 17-foot Waterline Restricted Class. However, William Fife designed one of them, called *Hatasoo*, and this boat seems to have killed the class off because 'she differed considerably in design from the other boats of the class and proved so fast that in any but very strong winds the destination of the first prize was practically a foregone conclusion.'

As so often happened elsewhere, a smaller club, the Innellan Corinthian Yacht Club, was started in 1895 'with the object of forming a class of small boats at moderate cost'. Despite these good intentions, the Innellan men could not agree among themselves on a single design. A division therefore took place, resulting in fourteen boats being built to plans by Peterson of Greenock and almost as many to a different design by Ninian of Largs. Two types of Innellan one-designs therefore sailed under the same burgee.

The rig of one of these 17-foot clinker-built keel boats was peculiar in that while the mainsail was sliding gunter, the mast was stepped so far forward in the boat as to resemble a cat rig, although a small jib was also set from a short bowsprit.

The Holy Loch Sailing Club, founded in 1895, also lost no time in establishing its own one-design class: a 16½-foot half-decker designed by Alfred Mylne. The sail area of 200 square feet meant that, besides the iron centre-plate, these little craft needed an additional 2-cwt of inside lead ballast.

On the east coast of Scotland, members of the Royal Tay Yacht Club decided in 1889 to form a one-design class from another Mylne design. Their boats, built by Gourlay Brothers of Dundee, were gaff-rigged sloops with a waterline length of 18 feet and considerable overhang. The class was known as the Seabirds, but they were quite unlike the West Lancashire Seabirds adopted by the Gourock Yacht Club. The 24-foot Gareloch OD and the Royal Forth OD, were similar boats, both designed by McGruer and both popular until a Dragon arrived on the Clyde in 1935, after which the Clyde feet of Gareloch ODs was sold away to Aldeburgh.

The International Dragon ODs are particularly interesting because, without ever having been intended as a one-design class, they quickly became one of the most successful of all international one-designs, being selected for seven Olympic Games up to 1972. Uffa Fox foresaw the potential of the Dragon Class in 1937 when he wrote: 'The Dragons have the qualities sought for in one-design classes. They will continue and prosper.'

The class originated almost sixty years ago, when the Royal Gothenburg Yacht Club in Sweden sponsored a competition-winning design by Johan Anker, a Norwegian, Anker had conceived a slim 29-foot yacht that proved to be 'just right' in the eyes of many people. The Clyde Dragon fleet was established in 1936 and by 1939 there were other fleets of Dragons at Ramsgate, in the Solent and in Northern Ireland. Plastic hulls and metal masts have replaced the original wood, making the craft less expensive to maintain. Dragons now race at Abersoch, Aldeburgh, Burnham, Cowes, Lowestoft, on the Medway and at Whitby.

As an alternative to the Dragon, in 1937 the Loch Long Sailing Club established a class of 21-foot keel boats based on another Norwegian design. Within a year there were eleven 'wee Dragons' on the Clyde, and soon after the Second World War the fleet increased to sixteen boats. There are fewer of them now in Scotland since some, like the Gareloch ODs, migrated to Aldeburgh in Suffolk.

For the most part, clubs in the West of England have tended to 'borrow' their one-design keel-boat classes by forming their own divisions of such yachts as the Bembridge Redwings and the Solent Sunbeams. An exception is the old Fowey Troy Class, in which the boats are straight-stemmed 18-footers, designed and built locally by A. H. Watty. With a draught of 3 feet 4 inches and a beam of only 6 feet, these bermuda-rigged keel boats are allowed a generous 298 square feet of sail.

There are also a number of indigenous dinghy classes distributed along the south-west coast, including the West of England OD, or Looe Redwing as it used to be called. This is a 14-foot open dinghy designed by Uffa Fox and resembling an early clinker-built 14-foot International. There is also the Dart OD, a 12-foot Morgan Giles design, started as a class in 1924 by the Royal Dart Yacht Club and also sailed by cadets from the Royal Naval College.

All the classes mentioned so far have been round-bilge designs, intended either for the clench (clinker) or the carvel methods of construction. However, two important American hard-chine designs reached the UK between the wars, and one became an Olympic class.

The Star One-Design dates back as far as 1911 in the United States, but it did not really catch on until after the First World War, by which time its original sliding-gunter mainsail had been replaced by the Marconi (bermuda) rig, albeit with an extraordinarily large mainsail and a very small jib. An International Star Association was formed in 1921 and in 1932 the Star was chosen for the Olympic Games, a choice that has been repeated for all subsequent Games except 1976. The hull of a Star is 22 feet 7½ inches overall and 15½ feet on the waterline, with a beam of 4½ feet at the chine and a draught of 3 feet 4 inches, using a cast-iron fin keel weighing 900 lbs. Stars have never been really popular in the UK, although there have been small fleets of them at Lowestoft, Burnham and Cowes.

The Snipe One-Design, like the Star, is hard-chined and three-quarter-decked, but being a centre-boarder and only 15½ feet overall it is more easily built and transported by an amateur. William Crosby, editor of the American magazine *The Rudder*, designed the Snipe and published the lines in 1931, having chosen hard-chine construction to encourage amateur building. In this he was successful: a fourteen-year-old boy built the first one and by 1939, of the 4000 boats in the class, half had been built by their owners. The Snipe was an immediate success and was soon adopted by many countries outside the US. A Snipe Class International Association was formed, and for a time the Snipe became the largest one-design class in the world.

In the UK the Snipe was more popular than the Star, and at one time there were Snipe fleets at Strangford Lough, Carrickfergus, Holyhead and Eastbourne as well as on the Blackwater and the Medway. However they now race mainly from clubs on the north Kent coast.

For a while, the 12-square-metre Sharpie achieved International status and was even chosen as an Olympic class in 1956. The design resulted from a competition in Germany in the 1920s and the hull is not unlike a duck punt, being 19 feet 7 inches long with a beam of 4½ feet and a draught of only a few inches with the plate up. The 125 square feet (12 square metres) of sail is made up of a sliding-gunter main on a short mast and a large overlapping jib. At one time or another there have been small fleets of these Sharpies on the Ouse, at Brancaster Staithe, at Burnham-on-Crouch and in Chichester Harbour.

Perhaps because the one-design movement began as a reaction against large expensive yachts, there have been relatively few one-designs that serve the dual purpose of racing and cruising. One of the earliest attempts to produce a racer-cruiser was made in 1923, with a boat designed by H. G. May of the Berthon Boat Co. of Lymington.

Craft of this type, which came to be known as the West Solent Restricted Class, were 34 feet overall with a waterline length of only 23 feet and a beam of 7½ feet. They drew 5 feet, had a fairly long keel and were allowed 567 square feet of sail. For a 34-foot yacht, the accommodation was very cramped by today's standards.

Another racer designed by Mylne in 1929, led to the formation of the Scottish Islands OD Class. The boat was 28 feet overall with a beam of 7 feet and a draught of 4½ feet. There were never more than about half a dozen of these auxiliary yachts, but they gave good racing right up to the 1960s.

The most successful wood-built one-design cruising class in the UK must be the South Coast One-Design. The SCOD was designed by Charles Nicholson in 1955 and the boats were built by Burnes of Bosham. The original requirement came from half a dozen members of the Island Sailing Club at Cowes, who wanted 'a cruising boat to sleep four people, which could be produced economically, be able to take part in coastal and Channel races and cruise safely in all expected weather conditions'. The yachts are 26 feet overall and 21 feet on the waterline. The beam is 7 feet 10 inches and they draw 5 feet 3 inches with a 2-ton ballast keel and a sail area of 281 square feet. That the SCODs live up to the specified requirements was demonstrated during the wild weather of Cowes Week 1985, after which *Yachts and Yachting* reported that 'seven out of eight races were sailed in weather that SCODs like best'.

To many, including some of the best helmsmen and yacht designers in the world, the merits of one-design racing are obvious. First and foremost, it is seen as a true test of personal skill and seamanship, for, as Manfred Curry wrote in his classic book, *Yachting Racing*: 'No other sport requires such versatility of talent and accomplishment as a sailing race; logical thinking; clear quick consideration; presence of mind; courage; endurance, often for hours at a time; keenness of observation; delicacy of feeling.'

For most of us, such a list of requirements is more than enough to make the sport interesting without our having to wonder whether that elaborately cut, expensive spinnaker was really worth the money. Nevertheless, some people argue that the one-design principle is bad, saying that it removes all incentive to develop and improve the performance of yachts. Taken to the extreme, this argument claims that if yacht racing had always been conducted under strict one-design constraints, we would still be sailing boats like the 'cod's head-and-mackerel-tail' Revenue cutters of the eighteenth century, since they were the fastest boats around when people first began to sail for pleasure.

It is true that improvements in the performance of one-design yachts have nearly always come from experiments made and experience gained in open-class racing. But it is equally true that different people race yachts to experience different kinds of satisfaction. Some are quite content to enjoy the subtle thrill that comes from handling a sailing boat well against competitors who are sailing the same kind of boat. Others are only really happy when they can see some way of changing the hull, the sails, the rig or equipment of their yacht in an attempt to make her go faster than their competitors' boats – before they too make the same alterations.

One thing is clear; for any one design class to remain healthy, its association or committee must review its regulations from time to time to decide whether more interest and enjoyment would result from some relaxation or modification of the rules, without incurring too much expense of jeopardising the chances of older boats. That old, wisely controlled one-design boats can continue to give great pleasure is seen each August when the 'X' boats compete in the Solent during Cowes Week, and in September when the RCODs and the RBODs race on the Crouch during Burnham Week. These famous classes exemplify the many thousands of small yachts that race against each other 'on equal terms' – the simple concept that was established almost a hundred years ago and has survived ever since.

7
IRENE OF
BRIDGWATER
Leslie Morrish

The development of rail and road transport put an end to Britain's dependence on water as a means of moving freight. The vast sailing fleets that had played such a vital role in this country's rapid industrial advance virtually disappeared, and today only a handful of the old vessels are still in existence. One of these is the Bridgwater ketch *Irene*.

It was in 1904 that Carver of Bridgwater in Somerset laid the keel of a 'new little ketch'. He took his time: repair work had priority and there was no eager would-be owner awaiting her completion. The ship's survival probably owed much to that measured approach for, as there was no deadline to meet, materials could be chosen with care and waited on as necessary. Wood was oiled repeatedly; fit was unhurried.

Shortly before her launch, the ketch was bought by Colthurst Symons, a local brick and tile manufacturer. Captain William Lee, her future master, was also part-owner. It was Gladys Symons who named the ketch *Irene* with the traditional bottle broken on the stem-post. It is not clear after whom the vessel was named, but many young ladies were later named after her – as was a street in Bridgwater. The *Irene* was launched on 29 May 1907, and the event was reported in the *Bridgwater Mercury* of 5 June:

Although Messrs F.J. Carver & Sons, the well-known Bridgwater Shipbuilder, have turned out many excellent vessels in the past, it is doubtful whether they have previously built a more shapely and graceful ship than *Irene*, which was successfully launched on Wednesday morning last. It is some years since a new craft was locally made, and consequently more than ordinary interest was taken in her launching proceedings. The *Irene* is a ketch of very smart and useful appearance, her dimensions being: length 85 feet; breadth 21 feet; and depth 9 feet; and she is registered to carry 165 tons. The *Irene*, which has been purchased by Messrs Clifford J. Symons (Taunton Road), Clifford Symons (Camden Road) and Captain Wm Lee (her future skipper), will be employed in the general trade of the port. The weather on Wednesday morning was chilly but bright, and large crowds assembled on both banks of the river to watch the launch – whilst numbers occupied points of vantage on the shipping, with which the river was fairly sprinkled. Photographers abounded, and many excellent snapshots of the vessel taking the water were secured. A considerable number of people were on the deck of the vessel, and the scene was one of considerable animation when just before eight o'clock the workmen removed the stays. A slight lift by a hydraulic jack at the vessel's bow caused the *Irene* to move, and she at once gracefully glided down the ways, saluting her future home with a generous splash, which caused a wave to wash the opposite bank, much to the discomfiture of those standing at the water's edge. The launch was in every way a complete success, and hearty cheers were raised as the *Irene* swung round to the tide and slowly drifted to the side of the *Sunshine*.

Colthurst Symons's bricks and tiles were the prime cargo out. It was clearly uneconomic simply to return in ballast and every effort was made to ensure a return cargo – corn, cattle feed, stone, scrap iron; on one occasion even live pigs. The voyages usually took in more than one port of call – for example, bricks would be taken to Swansea, coal from Swansea to Cork, iron to Milford Haven, the vessel might be in ballast to Charlestown, china clay would be transported to the Mersey and a mixed cargo back to Bridgwater. *Irene* was, on occasion, away for months at a time.

Cargo could be taken aboard and discharged with the help of a loading gaff which was carried on deck. With the ship's boat resting on the rail and the hatch covers removed, the gaff was rigged on the

Below: Launch of the *Irene* at Bridgwater in May 1907

mainmast. A single block on the gaff carried a line from the basket in the hold to the dolly winch abaft the mainmast. The basket was filled and lifted above the hatch-coamings, then the gaff was swung over and the basket emptied into the waiting horse and cart. Often, however, every one of the *Irene*'s 165 back-breaking tons was handed by the crew alone. In tidal creeks a gangplank could be rigged to the bank and along this sacks of cattle feed were carried on shoulders or bricks wheeled in barrows. An easy run down with the tide in would become, as the water receded, a wearisome climb for tired men.

Speed was often important. To discharge on a beach at low water and sail off on the next tide could be vital if wind and sea were changing. At such times the winch was discarded and instead the cargo was 'jumped' out. A climbing frame of oars or spars was lashed up; three men at a time would climb up the frame, seize a line rove through a higher block, and jump off. Their weight raised the load up. It was swung out and over the side, while another basket was filled below. The men would then climb the frame again . . . and again.

Yet it would be misleading to picture life aboard such a vessel as the *Irene* as unrelenting toil. With the cargo stowed and sails hoisted, the crew could relax – indeed, summer cruises became family holidays.

Carrying freight across the Bristol Channel from Wales to the north coast of Somerset, Devon and Cornwall was one area where coastal water transport remained competitive as it became less viable elsewhere. Not that the *Irene* was confined there – she made many fast passages to the Clyde, to the south coast and on to London. As road and rail links improved, she turned increasingly to Ireland. Ships that flew the red ensign were in a delicate position in those days of the 'troubles' and *Irene* was in more danger from trigger-happy combatants than ever she faced at sea. During over fifty years of commercial life, *Irene* was never in a serious mishap. The wisdom and experience of her masters must have been a major factor, but those who know the ship well suspect a charmed life, a magic, a smile of the gods. Certainly her luck has held in the twenty-five years since her retirement from commerce – despite exposure to neglect, abuse and some dubious seamanship.

As sail power declined in importance, *Irene*'s owners succumbed to the inevitable. *Irene* had to be profitable. Although the engine room and fuel took up precious space and engines themselves were expensive, they were becoming more reliable and made a ship less dependent on wind and harbour towing services. Commercial considerations had determined *Irene*'s launch without an engine; and it was commercial

Above: Captain Bill Schiller (right), master of the *Irene* from 1938 to 1959

consideration that, after twelve years, led to its installation.

In 1919, a 40 hp Invincible changed *Irene*'s label from 'SV' (Sailing Vessel) to the then coveted 'MV' (Motor Vessel). The engine proved its worth so well that in 1923 it was made redundant in favour of a 70 hp Bollinder. After sixteen years this was in turn replaced by a 90 hp Ellwe.

Once she had been given the Ellwe engine, the *Irene* was independent of her sails. A full rig meant a full crew of six, and men were rarer and more expensive in the 1940s than when the ship was launched. Thus finance dictated that her lofty rigging be pruned – and down came the topmast; off came 16 feet of bowsprit; the mizzen gaff was discarded; the crew was halved. The *Irene* was now a sail-assisted motor vessel.

The butchery was justified, however, for *Irene* remained profitable for many more years. The nature of her cargo changed: brick and tile manufacture was dying in Bridgwater, and by this time rail links with Bristol and beyond were well established. So *Irene* moved down the peninsula to Bideford to trade from there, until she was laid up in 1960.

Sold and resold three times, *Irene* was then sailed round to the River Hamble. Conversion to a yacht was put in hand by the construction of a monstrous deck cabin and wheelhouse over the main hatch. But the owner lost interest, and after his death *Irene* was again up for sale. She was neglected: her paint was peeling, her wood greening and her price dropping. In 1966 she became mine – for £2,000.

I bought *Irene* with the intention of making her a London home. Her attraction as a houseboat on the Thames was enhanced by the possibility of taking her out to sea as well. At the time I had no concept of her historic value, no idea that she was unique. It was only later I learnt that the National Maritime Museum had reluctantly turned her down because of the cost of preservation, that the Exeter Maritime Museum were angling feverishly to purchase her, that there were articles about her in the history books. I just loved her.

The project started on the worst possible footing: £2,000 of borrowed money; another £700 of marine mortgage to prime the restoration fund; and a starry-eyed landlubber, his head full of cottonwool, in charge of this precious fragment of Britain's history. But we worked weekends and holidays for six months to stop the tide of decay, refurbish the steering gear and reassemble the engine. Then, on a windless weekend in June 1966, we motored to the Thames. At Tilbury the masts were drawn and laid on the deck.

The bridges of London have an air-draught (the space between the top of the arch and the height of the water at high water, spring tide) of 18–19 feet – all the bridges, that is, except Hammersmith. The clearance there measures just 14 feet. Whether this was by design, an innumerate builder, stretch in the suspension cables or subsidence in West London, Hammersmith Bridge is the bane of the Thames waterman.

Irene motored happily under the other bridges with the help of a big spring tide. The air-gauge at Hammersmith registered 17 feet. Our bowsprit was 15½ feet above the waterline measured at anchor; we should have known it would be more with the ship under power. The bowsprit slipped neatly under the centre of the arch, tapped its way along the centre girder and drove upwards through the pavement. The spar fractured at the stem-post and we stormed on under a shower of fragments.

Irene heralded her London advent in grand style: the bridge carried a gas main and we had cracked it. It was rush hour and the bridge had to be closed; gas supplies to 10,000 homes in South London were cut off.

For the next ten years *Irene* was primarily a houseboat. The hold was slowly transformed into a home of singular elegance and comfort. The fo'c'sle accommodation, ripped out when the crew was cut down, was now rebuilt as the children's bedroom. Abaft of that was the master cabin, the heads and a bathroom. Behind that again was the large saloon, with a spiral staircase, a grand piano, an organ and a dining table that dispensed with chairs by being sunk into a well in the lower deck. The saloon stretched back to the galley and a laundry room; abaft of that was the engine room.

The deck cabin was retained. It was ill-proportioned, incomplete and in the way, but it was a delightful sun-lounge. The southern view from our Brentford berth was over the river, the bird sanctuary island and Kew Gardens. One could always pull the curtains on the other side to blot out the gasworks.

But the *Irene* was not just to be a houseboat. We rerigged her. The bowsprit was replaced with a longer spar and the masts were put in tabernacles – steel mast cases – stepped on to the keelson. In that way the masts could be lowered to get under the bridges – even Hammersmith. We rebuilt the hounds, the cross-trees and trestle-trees on the mainmast and rehoused a tall topmast. Sails were made – canvas roped with hemp – and we worked on the engine.

The Ellwe engine was 5 tons of brass and cast-iron trouble. We must have invested a yearful of man-hours on that malignant misanthrope. There was a school of thought, which I shared, that once the brute was put right it would run forever. For thirteen years I held that creed, while the only reliable feature of that machine was its unreliability. But it was my education in seamanship. Every manoeuvre, every decision, every technique of sailing had to be performed in the knowledge that the Ellwe was likely to choose the critical moment to stop.

We learnt to use the tide, to tweak the best from the sails, to creep into wind, to scandalise the peak. We learnt to turn on the anchor and to sail off it, to use the anchor to drudge in a tidal flow. We learnt the value of the kedge to haul the vessel out of trouble and, of course, we learnt the techniques of being towed.

It is sad, though inevitable, that harbours are no longer geared for motorless craft. No eager hufflers wait to help the crew warp the vessel to or from her mooring. No strategic posts or bollards are there for a line taken by the gig. No oarsmen heave their work boat through the harbour entrance tugging behind a helpless monster. Instead there is the impatient rasp of the tanker's radio: 'Doesn't that sailing boat have an engine?'

A mud berth in tidal water is not ideal for any vessel – even one designed to take the ground. *Irene* tolerated the conditions at Brentford for ten years until my need for a London home disappeared, and then she was freed into deep water. In 1980 it was agreed she should return to the Bristol Channel. The Ellwe was replaced with a Gardner 6LX –

secondhand out of a cement lorry, but reliable power at the press of a button.

We spent an idyllic season: we pottered along the south coast in timorous hops from port to anchorage; we ventured out in gentle winds and rarely lost sight of land.

The Gardner transformed our experience of the *Irene*. Suddenly I could promise to leave on a particular tide, to arrive at a certain port. I could negotiate narrow water crowded with expensive plastic. I could even leave harbour without reducing the harbour master to agonised fury. Best of all, the engine gave us the freedom to sail. Yet even today we use the engine as little as possible, and diesel oil is used with the same reverent frugality as a good malt – in truth, the fuel tank isn't much bigger than the booze cupboard.

By 1981 *Irene* had reached her home waters, where she was greeted with a gale of wind. She tore up the channel from Bideford Bay with a swift spring tide. We arrived too soon – shallow water, tide at half-flood and a lee shore – so I tried to reach the sanctuary of Watchet harbour. With the sails down and the engine stemming the flood, we crabbed slowly towards the harbour entrance. There was little water beneath us and some wicked rocks on our port quarter. It was clearly a hazardous exercise and I decided to motor back to deeper water. At that moment our apprentice engineer decided that the Gardner was about to seize and he cut the engine. It was not time to argue, it was time to thank the Ellwe for the training its unreliability had given me.

The staysail halliard smoked through the blocks and with a brief tweak of the clew to port, the ship's head pointed to open water. Sail and wheel to starboard, *Irene* clawed herself off a lee shore where gale-driven waves fragmented on the rocks at the cliff foot.

The apprentice's diagnosis proved wrong: a spare battery had fallen over, spilling acid and filling the engine room with smoke. Fortunately, the Gardner itself was fine, and its reassuring purr allayed our remaining concerns. Watchet was not now possible – a mile and more uptide and upwind – leaving the River Parrett as the escape route from the shoal-strewn Bridgwater Bay. We were a tide early for the television cameras that were intended to record our triumphant arrival, but that seemed to us a trivial consideration compared with the relief of sanctuary.

For four weeks *Irene* basked in the Parrett, downstream from where she had been launched seventy-three years before. Our final goal was Bristol, where there was a deep-water berth as well as the facilities needed for the next step in *Irene*'s career.

It was quite apparent that the amateurish scratching of the previous fourteen years had done little more than stem the ship's decay. It was time to adopt a new professional approach. In this the good fortune of the *Irene* held: we found John Woolley, one of the few master craftsmen knowledgeable in the structure of such vessels. If *Irene* were to become once more a serious sailing machine, she would need extensive renovation. It was not until we embarked on the project that we began to realise just how extensive – in fact, it proved to be almost a rebuild from the waterline.

Irene had been framed in oak and planked with pitch pine; keel and garboard strake were of elm and the keelson of greenheart. Galvanised black iron was used to fasten her throughout. Construction like that could last forever. But the upper planks on the side of the ship were different. In harbour the vessel could be subject to rough handling – with a granite quay on one side, a heavily laden iron freighter on the other and a swell from the harbour mouth, the vessel could be hammered.

The four top strakes and the covering board (the wide timber at the edge of the deck) were therefore made of harder wood. Strakes two and three were of greenheart – wood so hard that nails would bend rather than penetrate – and this had taken well the abuse of the years. Covering board, strakes one and four were chestnut – poor man's oak. That too had withstood the battering, but had succumbed to rainwater, arch-enemy of wooden ships. The chestnut was badly decayed.

Oak stanchions were built through the covering board. Where they touched the rain-sodden chestnut, they too had rotted. Water dripped through on to the end grain of the oak frames – the upper timber there, the futtock, was softened. And water dripped on to the beam ends, slowly turning solid oak into detritus.

All affected timber had to be replaced. There are times when it is reasonable to cut back to good wood and scarf a new section on to the old. But the affected areas here were widespread and scattered. It would have been a patchy and inadequate bodge to deal with it piecemeal. The task was further extended by the need to gain access – good wood would also have to be sacrificed. In order to replace the deck beams, it was necessary to cut away the deck. To fasten the new futtocks, the greenheart strakes fell to the chainsaw. To replace the stanchions, the main and the topgallant rails had to go.

With the decision to rip up the deck, it was clearly opportune to remove the deck cabin. It had outlived its usefulness and was discarded without regret. The useful timber, including the entire roof, was carefully stored – indeed, the cabin roof was used to protect our pile of valuable wood.

Irene doesn't seem to suffer from the interest of thieves. Tools do disappear, but often enough they turn up again where the user had left them, or perhaps a penitent shipwright paints a dramatic tale of a failed grasp, a fumble, a frantic grab and a splash. I am unable to claim of any single object that it was certainly stolen – except the cabin roof. It measured 18 × 12 feet and took six men to lift it. One murky night it disappeared.

The cabin had been built over the main hatch. That hatch itself was an enlargement of the original. We decided to replace it as Carver had designed: genuine and functional with coamings, hatch boards, canvas cover and battens. In one corner a booby hatch gave access to a spiral staircase into the hold. *Irene*'s days as a transporter of cargo were over, but the hatch was useful if only for loading gear such as the piano or the freezer. In addition, by building removable decking within the hatch at deck level, we gained much invaluable storage space.

The anchor windlass had taken a good deal of punishment over the years: the snatch of an anchor that did not reach bottom, the repetitious wrench when the vessel was bucking in a seaway, and the rainwater creeping into cracks and shakes. It had suffered, too, at the hands of the pruners. When the tall rig was cut back in the 1940s and the crew halved, master, mate and seaman slept aft – behind and above the engine room. The fo'c'sle cabin was redundant and the space became part of the cargo hold. The massive windlass bitts, the main support of the barrel, had extended through the cabin and been housed in the beams of the fo'c'sle floor. These timbers were cut back to the deck-head and the long leverage that prevented forward movement was lost. The ironwork of the moving parts, however, was essentially sound.

It was clear, then, that the time had come to rebuild the windlass. The iron was sand-blasted and machined; bearings were fitted and the wood renewed entire. The bitts were taken through to the inner lining of the ship deep by the keel.

In her early days, *Irene* had had a whaleback. This was an enclosed superstructure abaft the wheel with a backward-curving roof, a lamp locker on one side and a loo on the other. The main purpose of the whaleback was protection. When the ship is running before a gale, waves overtake it. The *Irene*'s wide counter helps keep her stern above water level. Where wave distance is long enough to allow the bow to burrow in the trough, there is no problem even when the vessel is deeply laden. With the shorter, steeper waves of shallower water, the bow can be raised at the same time as the stern and the wave breaks over the ship. She is 'pooped', but the whaleback protects the helmsman from being washed away.

When the *Irene* became a motor vessel the whaleback was dismantled. So, too, was the skylight above the master's cabin. Instead the engine room was raised above bulwark level and the master's cabin extended upwards to compensate for the encroachment of engine space. An enclosed wheelhouse was built to shelter the helmsman. Before the time of *Irene*'s major renovation, however, this whole structure had badly rotted and finally collapsed. We had rebuilt and extended the master's cabin by erecting a deckhouse over the engine room, but that left the wheel open and unprotected. An enclosed wheelhouse is not ideal for a sailing vessel; it seemed much more sensible to rebuild the whaleback.

This was constructed with an extended roof and side walls to give the helm a little weather protection. The main part behind the wheel was enclosed to form a chart room. The skylight was also rebuilt, but placed forward of the mizzenmast to light and ventilate the galley.

Meanwhile, the main reconstructive work on the hull progressed. Exposed areas were fully cleaned and soaked with linseed oil and preservatives. End grain was painted with red lead and protected with barge felt. Futtocks and stanchions were cut from baulks of oak – those near the stern had curve that needed similar contour in the grain of the timber. New hull planking was carefully sculpted from some old pitch pine which we had been very fortunate to pick up from a dismantled warehouse in Wales in the form of beams 40 feet long and 14 inches square. Deck beams were removed and replaced with new oak, one by one, to ensure that the shape of the hull was not affected, and deck planking was replaced in pitch pine. We used oakum to caulk the seams, paint putty to pay the hull and pitch for the deck. Rails and bulwarks were also replaced.

'Fold-away' masts are not ideal for a deep-sea vessel. *Irene*'s masts were in any case in poor shape, so we went to the Forest of Dean, chose two magnificent Douglas firs and took them back to Bristol.

The construction of a round spar from a round tree is not as straightforward as it seems. A tree's most recent few years' growth is sapwood and has to be cut away. The taper in a mast is cigar-shaped and precisely formulated, and irregularities in straightness and thickness can easily be transferred from tree to spar. To transform it into a mast the tree is first adzed and planed to a square cross-section and shaped to the correct diameters to give the right taper. The square is then made octagonal, then given sixteen even sides and finally rounded. So it was that we built mainmast and mizzenmast for *Irene*, 60 feet long with a given diameter of 15 and 14 inches. Massive oak cheeks were attached at the hounds to take the downward pull of the standing rigging, and ironwork in the form of rings, throat crane and mast-cap were fitted.

The trees had been felled in November and the masts were stepped in April. That meant that the wood was not seasoned. To compensate we soaked them extensively in linseed oil and Cuprinol; end grain was well sealed, shakes filled with tallow and a long hole was drilled vertically down from the mast-head, filled with oil and plugged. Slowly the oil soaks its way right down the core; old sailors maintained that they could always recognise masts treated in this way because they were easier to scrape.

The rigging was overhauled but little was replaced. The shrouds were heavy-duty iron rope that had suffered negligibly over the years. Running rigging was man-made 'hemp'.

The *Irene* was at last back in one piece, much to my delight and much to the disconcertion of the wharf-side Jeremiahs. It was now time to move to Gloucester to dry dock, partly to facilitate survey, partly to give the bottom the 'full treatment' instead of the quick between-tide slap-on. It was also to deal with the keel.

The most significant mishap to the *Irene* occurred in the late 1940s when she grounded in fog on Breaksea rocks. The forefoot of the keel had been chewed up and been replaced in Harris's yard in Appledore. That repair was now itself badly worn and crumbled, with the near-twice-daily groundings of a further forty years. Now, with the weight transferred to lateral shores and a hydraulic jack at the stem, the forward 30 feet of keel was replaced in elm. However, although adequate, the job was not satisfactory. What became apparent was that the whole keel was badly eroded – indeed, the vessel's draught was a full 6 inches less than her marks indicated.

The propellor shaft was the other area of concern. *Irene* had a very fine run; she tapered aft to a stern-post of some 10 inches. She had not been built with an engine in mind and when a 6-inch stern-tube was drilled through deadwood and post, it left but 2 inches of timber on either side. Heavy iron plating helped to compensate for the resulting weakness, but constant movement and wear had over the years led to vibration, thereby causing loosening and leaks.

It was clearly wise to remove the propellor from a central position, replace and strengthen the weakened areas and close the screw aperture in front of the rudder. Long straight keels turn badly when the rudder's effectiveness is reduced by a leakage through such a huge hole – the propellor was 41 inches across. Much work would have to be done to plan for such a venture – if not a central propellor, should one opt for a wing-prop or twins – and if so, how should they be driven?

In the meantime, our basic rebuild was completed in time for a drunken celebration on 29 May 1982: the *Irene* was seventy-five years old. It was a further two years before the ship returned to dry dock to replace the keel entire, to remove the central propellor, to rebuild the stern-post deadwood and rudder and to install twin folding hydraulically driven propellors.

Since her seventy-fifth birthday *Irene* has embarked on a new career. A Sailing Society has been formed to enable enthusiasts to help preserve and sail her. Anyone can join for a modest £3 per annum (see page 159) and is thereby entitled to receive periodic newsletters, to paint, scrape and hump ballast and to take the opportunity to sail. The sailing programme is extensive and varied: a weekend in the Bristol Channel or the Tall Ships' Race to Lisbon; a cruise for divers in the Scottish Islands or a rally for traditional ships in the Baltic.

Irene is safe and sea-kindly, but few voyages are without their moments. A leisurely jaunt down to the Channel Islands was changed to drama when, with two anchors down in a sheltered bay, we dragged before a whole gale. With rocks to lee of us, we sailed away under two headsails, main and reefed mizzen. We grazed past jagged outcrops to catch the Alderney Race, and on into the English Channel. A full moon, a huge beam sea, and *Irene* tore up the miles with spray drenching the mainsail 30 feet above our heads.

Once, when she was tied up in Watchet harbour, a westerly storm created a swell that threw the ship around as if she were a dinghy. We escaped on engine and staysail, but at the harbour mouth a propellor fouled, so we sailed on under staysail alone. Five knots through the water with 55 knots of wind brought us to the Avon too early in the tide to enter Bristol.

We were in the Scilly Islands the time we relied on the plastic depth sounder, misread feet for fathoms and dropped the anchor in 'shallow water'. It dangled uselessly, many feet from the bottom, as the tide swept us towards an evil reef. My condemnation of plastic was under-

Opposite: Quiet moments on the *Irene*

mined when the plastic engine starter button spirited us out of danger.

Then there was the occasion in Cumberland Dock, when *Irene* was slow astern and inching towards the quay. An impatient sailor stood on the rail at the stern and jumped prematurely. His feet slipped on the brightwork and his leap was short. For a moment he hung on the edge of the wharf with the ship's counter approaching and threatening to crush him. Then he fell. As he hit the water the propellors were in full ahead, pushing him away from danger and prising open the wharf/*Irene* nutcracker. A bow-line and a few heavies delivered a damp but unabashed mariner back on deck.

There are other moments, too: sun-bathing in a soft southerly breeze with all sail up and the slap of water upon hull to induce drowsy serenity; when the end of the dog-watch is heralded by the savours of the galley and a bottle of good wine bought cheaply from a Calais supermarket is enjoyed with English beef roasted rare; when a leisurely row in a laden dinghy from a secluded anchorage fills the local pub with us aliens before we return mellow.

Yet distant waters lure. The label 'coaster' or 'coasting freighter' is misleading, for it applies more to the use to which the vessel is put than to her capabilities. (A delivery van, for instance, might never leave its home town but still be capable of driving across a continent.) The sea that a coaster has to survive is qualitatively little different from that faced by the deep-water freighter. As the ocean bed shelves, the long roller is moulded into shorter, steeper waves, so a shorter hull is under less strain; the deep-sea vessel is bigger primarily because long distances are better served economically by bulk carriers.

The coastal craft needs to beat round headlands and off lee shores, so the windward performance of the fore-and-aft rig is preferred. The ocean carrier travels great distances in favourable winds and is better served by the powerful squaresails. These distinctions are slight, however: many large square-riggers coasted and many small fore-and-afters plied with Newfoundland. Certainly the distinctions create no argument against the *Irene*'s freedom to sail far afield. What is in question is the nature of conservation.

Irene was built and launched as a ketch. Over the years vessels had their rig changed according to the needs and tastes of their masters, and *Irene* was no exception. Our principle has been to restore her rig to original. The ketch rig is well designed for tight manoeuvres in narrow waters by a small crew. But if the ship is to carry a larger crew in deep water, do we violate a principle of conservation by adding squaresails?

Irene is now to cross yards on the forward mast. Her label will have to change to 'topsail ketch' or even 'brigantine'. But she will be better suited to ocean sailing. She will provide more experience aloft for her crew. She will be more alluring to film companies in their quest to recreate the past. She will qualify for the Australian Bicentennial re-enactment of the voyage of eleven British merchantment carrying emigrants and convicts to settle and found a nation. No vessel deserves more to be chosen for this adventure. As the last and only working representative of the British merchant navy in the days of sail, the *Irene* will be sailing to the other side of the world in 1987.

Below: *Irene* sailing under her restored ketch rig

8
AN OLD MAN OF THE SEA
Tom Salmon

I had seen *Our Daddy* at sea once or twice, but more often as she
rounded that Cornish granite harbour arm at Looe flying pennants
parading the fact that she had shark aboard – a Cornish fishing boat in
the truest of her settings, the only old-time Looe lugger (her regist-
ration number is in single figures: FY7) still regularly sailing out of her
home port, and as well-founded now as when she was built in 1921. Yet
I'd never *walked* her until one day in spring 1985, when she lay on a
falling tide alongside the wall just below the finely arched bridge that
joins East and West Looe.

I walked *Our Daddy* with 'A.J.' – Alfred John Pengelly, whose
grandfather had built her and whose family had sailed her ever since,
fishing the waters of Mount's Bay to the south and the Eddystone Light
and beyond to the east. We went down the seaweeded steel ladder (he
twenty years my senior, but much more agile) and we stood on the deck,
and for the briefest of moments – for A.J. is the most welcoming of
fellows – I suddenly felt that I was not there at all. It was just a man and
a boat, and a sharing of something quite special across a fishing lifetime.

Alfred John Pengelly, BEM, is arguably the most respected fisherman that Cornwall, in relatively recent years, has ever known. This is
partly because he could *talk* – quietly and persuasively, in a soft
Cornish burr – in places which would have inhibited many of his fellow
fishermen, even though they shared his inherent qualities of honesty
and directness. Most fishermen are good on quays but few relish council
chambers. A.J., however, seemed not to mind – and I remember still,
as a young local-newspaper reporter in the early 1950s, watching him at
meetings of the Cornwall Sea Fisheries Committee. Even in my inex-
perienced callowness, I realised that when he spoke I was listening to
the authentic voice of Cornish fishing. Not only could he talk fishing,
but he could also fish alongside the very best fishermen who ever sailed
from any Cornish port.

A few years back, A.J. retired from an active fishing life, as befits a

Above: A. J. Pengelly in the crew's quarters on *Our Daddy*

man even of his seemingly youthful eighty years – although a day's shark fishing never seems to go amiss – and wrote the story of his life. He called it *Oh, For a Fisherman's Life*, a title which seemed exactly right for the man, his quite special love and knowledge of the sea and the skills he so patiently learned about the harvesting of it. It is a book which gives a clear impression, in a way that many more sophisticated writers do not, of what life was like in the fishing industry of Cornwall in the changing years of this century and also in the villages around the coast where the fishermen lived.

In this acount of fishing out of Looe – though I doubt it would differ much had it been about Mevagissey or Polperro – I have drawn upon A.J.'s own writings, upon a friendship that means much to me, upon chats that we've had together over the years (interviews for various BBC programmes among them); and also upon an interview that A.J. gave for the *Under Sail* programme.

Our Daddy was built for A.J.'s grandfather by a boat builder called Richard Pearce and named to Mr Pengelly's taste in a tradition that underlines the family feeling so esteemed by the fishermen of Looe.

They lived, these fishing families, in the lower part of the town, in cottages that huddled together in a caring and sharing community. As A.J. recalls, Mrs Mutton, in the little grocer's shop, more than once handed over groceries which could not be paid for until the weather eased and the fishing fleet went to sea again. In those days, too – it was the 1920s – the fishermen's wives brought dinners to be cooked in communal ovens in the village bakehouse. These might be potted pilchards or marinated fish as the Cornish women described them – a taste which lingers even today on middle-aged Cornish palates; or fish pies, made at home with vegetables from plots of ground the fishermen were allowed to use.

The pilchards were preserved in salt in summer in huge earthenware jars, to be brought out in the stormy winter months, laced with spices, bay leaves and vinegar and simmered the whole night through.

The names of the luggers of Looe read like a litany of the given names of Looe's fishing families: *Beatrice Ann, Olive, Henrietta, Florie, Myrtle, Victoria* and *Eliza Jane*. There is no doubt at all that the fishermen of this Cornish town wish to sail in the company of their loved ones. Occasionally the names enshrined on the boats of the Looe fishing fleet emphasised the deep religious convictions of the men who sailed in them – for example, the *John Wesley* (FY 35) – and there were skippers who liked to recall at sea the hymns they sang in Cornish chapels when they were ashore. Thus the *Kindly Light* sailed out of Looe, and the *Onward*, and the *Guide Me* – fishing-boat names redolent of the evangelical tunes that mean as much to the Cornish as they do to the Welsh. There was even one Looe lugger christened *Billy Bray* after a drunken Cornishman who saw the light and danced with the joy of his new-found Methodism across the scarred mining landscape of the county to convert many sinners.

The Pengellys, however, named their vessels to remind them of family ties. Already they had two luggers called *Our Boys* and *Our Girls*, and A.J.'s grandfather was much of the mind that he should be remembered too; hence the origin of his new vessel's name. 'The *Our Daddy* will be sailing long after I've gone,' he said.

Our Daddy was built a little bigger than most luggers of her time. She was 44½ feet overall and 13½ feet in the beam, with a draught of more than 6 feet. Mr Pengelly hoped that her larger-than-average capacity would help him avoid the problems faced by certain other Looe luggers. He had seen them quite incapable of taking on board the heavy catches of fish entangled in their huge drift-nets, up to a mile long, that they shot through the nights into dark Cornish seas. The pause in fishing during the First World War had led to an enormous replenishment of fish stocks, and there were times, merely for the safety of the boats and the crews, that the nets had to be cut adrift. There was simply no hope

Above: Luggers at the Looe quayside in the 1930s

of being able to carry the catch, even if it had been brought aboard.

In October 1921 *Our Daddy* was launched. Sail was her essential fishing aid and even today sail keeps her exactly where her skipper wants her to be. But she did have two modest engines, one of 13 hp and the other 7 hp. She also had a cabin which could cater for five just this side of comfort, and a coal-fired cooking stove. A.J. joined her for her first winter's fishing. His father was the skipper; his father's brother Ernest was the engineer; there were two others who were the crew; and A.J. was the cook – and seasick for most of the time.

Alfred John Pengelly was born in the Cornish fishing village of Looe in 1906. He weighed, as he's fond of telling, only 4½lbs. At the tender age of four he was so aggrieved (the Cornish dialect for it is 'mazed') that his family would not allow him to go to sea with them that he stood on

Above: Preparing *Our Daddy* for a new fishing season

the harbour arm and threw pebbles at them as they sailed out! With fishing so much a part of his family's life, it was hardly surprising that the young Alfred John wanted to go to sea, or that, even at four, he should have realised that that was where his future would lie.

There once were days – and they were talked about to such boys as the young A.J., not only in their bare little primary schools but also around the supper table at home – when 2000 and more Cornishmen earned their livelihood from the sea. These men ran their tiny boats deep into the North and Irish Seas, and returned to tucked-away harbours so wind-lashed and tide-bound that their womenfolk would throw ropes to them to make their coming home secure. There were pilchards then, which swarmed in their hundreds of thousands into the Cornish fishing grounds, and, way back, so important was the role of Looe in harvesting this marine wealth that a Charles II Looe 'token' was minted depicting a pilchard, so that this fish came to be known as a 'Looe trout'. The whole of Looe breathed fishing – from the boats which came and went from the harbour to the fish cellars where the women worked, packing and preserving the catches, and gossiping all the while.

Over the last decade or so, fishing in Cornwall has changed more dramatically than at any other time in its history. In the 1970s and 1980s bigger ships have come into what were always regarded as essentially

Cornish waters – multi-national vessels towing vast encircling seine-nets and ferrying their bulging catches to huge 'mother ships' which wait in Cornish bays. Sail to them is a thing of the past; diesel has taken over, and fish stocks have been decimated.

Yet, in A.J.'s own lifetime, there were occasions when not even sail was needed to harvest the sea. All you did was row out into the bay off Looe and trail nets behind you to encircle vast shoals. These were the dying days of Cornwall's seine-net fishery, and, as a boy, A.J. was more than once an excited part of it. 'Mackerel's up!' was a cry he still remembers; and he remembers, too, the last of the mackerel seine boats, 30 or so feet long and trailing a net of a quarter of a mile. The rowers listened to the shouts of the 'huer', a fishermen himself, up on the cliffs directing the boatmen to shoals which ruffled the surface of the water as if a wayward breeze had selected one special part of the sea in which to play.

'In those days,' A.J. told me once, 'you would think that the mackerel wanted to give themselves up. You could see them driving towards the shore.' (There was, incidentally, a joke in Looe about mackerel money in those days. It was said that the owner of a boat threw the money for the catch towards the top of an upright ladder, and what rested on the rungs was the crew's share!)

Such memories belong to A.J.'s earliest youth, when he watched rather than took part in the industry which was to become his way of life. For him much of that life was to be under sail – without radar and similar fishing aids, and dependent upon men who could read the signs of nature as easily and naturally as the rest of us read road signs.

A.J. went to sea the moment he left school – at the age of fourteen, in 1920. There were forty-five luggers in Looe then, as well as many other small fishing boats, and he joined his father who was the skipper of the *Sweet Home*. The luggers were long-lining: their lines trailed 3 miles and more from the stern of the boat at night as they fished the grounds off the Lizard and outside the Eddystone Light. On the way out they netted pilchards for bait, and it was the boy's job to help cut them up. There was never an idle moment aboard a fishing boat, from the time it left harbour to the time it returned. But A.J.'s trouble – and could there be a worse one for a young man desperate to become a fisherman? – was his chronic proneness to seasickness. Whether the weather was fine or rough, he was sick. Once, he recalls, he was even sick before the boat set sail, and after three months of it his father sorrowfully told him, 'You will never make a fisherman.'

So, at a wage of 2s 6d (12½p) a week, he became a shipwright's apprentice in a West Looe boatyard and helped, in a learning way, to build the *Eileen*, a Looe lugger of the kind he pined to be sailing himself. By then *Our Daddy* had been built, and the lure of her was too much for the young boat builder's apprentice. He joined her for a winter season, then endured another three years of seasickness, but finally got over it and became what he had always wished to be – a fisherman.

On the deck of *Our Daddy* that spring in 1985, A.J. told me a little about what fishing under sail all those years ago was like: the way the men around him took and held their boats precisely in the places they should be, the way they read the signs of sea and sky, and the pride they had in a calling which, while it never provided a lush living, drew on the skills they had learned from their forebears and which they felt to be a badge of their trade.

A.J. described the night fishing in Mount's Bay long ago: 'There were lights,' he said, 'lights all round. It was like a city out there. But the lights came from boats and not from houses'.

He then went on to talk about the traditional methods:

> Much of it was under sail up to the 1930s and into them – even the Brixham and Plymouth trawlers. And the grounds were good, too: they'd been rested in the War years. There were no electronics. You learned the fishing grounds from your father and grandfather, and that's the way you were trained into it. All we had was a compass and our own heads. But we knew about tides and drifts, and we used our eyes, and we watched the colour of the water and the gannets and the seagulls diving. And some things were funny, you know. We always used to reckon that the winter fishing would start on 5 November, and that's when it did. You could look out, and see signs of the fish coming – and that's when we always started.
>
> We had a little motor power – not much, but enough to take us through. But very often we shut the engines off and drifted under sail. You could *hear* things then. You could hear the fish playing on the top of the water. We used to say they 'rattled'. And then the skipper would turn the boat into the wind and shoot the nets before the wind into the shoal of fish. The least vibration, especially an engine noise, would scatter the shoal. That's the way we used to fish in those days, until all this new apparatus came in, and did away, in my opinion, with the *challenge* of fishing. I won't say that fishermen now aren't good fishermen. They are. But if there are fish about, they can *see* them in the wheelhouse: they can see the depth of them, and they can nearly count how many there are. It's *different*, isn't it?

Of all the changes A.J. has seen in his industry, the most drastic is surely the death of sail. In his time, the ability to sail and to master the wind was a paramount part of a fisherman's apprenticeship; and the

Opposite: A.J. crewed on the J-class *Astra* during the 1928 racing season

young men of Looe, as in other fishing ports around the Cornish coast, discovered that their skill in sail could bring them summertime wages to augment winter earnings from fishing. Between the Wars in particular, wealthy men indulged themselves in the ownership of some of the most lovely pleasure-sailing and competitive yachts that have ever been built, and they would employ local fishermen to crew for them.

In the spring of 1927 A.J. received a telegram enquiring whether he would join the crew of the *Paula*, a 15-metre racing yacht at Burnham-on-Crouch. A year later he was invited to join the new big yacht *Astra*.

The *Astra* was a beauty. Built for Sir Mortimer Singer, she was a bermudan cutter, 100 feet long with a mast of 130 feet. To sail her properly required a crew of eighteen, and when her skipper came to select his men he turned to the sailing skills of fishermen. There were men from the West Mersey and Whitstable, Plymouth, Brixham and Southampton – and, from the wages they were paid, '5 shillings (25p) a week is to be taken out to ensure good conduct, the whole payable at the end of the season'.

The season was long and varied, and the regime was relentless: up at 6.30am, a cup of tea, then scrubbing the deck and polishing the brass; breakfast at 8.30; and if things went well, the next meal would be supper at 5pm or thereabouts, when the *Astra* was squared-up at anchor and the day's racing done. For all the hard work, however – and no fisherman a stranger to that – there were pleasures, too, not the least of them working sails that spread like clouds, employing skills they had mastered in other waters.

Expectations were different in those days. 'I pay tribute', writes A.J. in his autobiography, 'to the owner of *Astra*. Sir Mortimer Singer was a very kind and considerate gentleman. Each week that we were racing, hampers of cakes were sent on board for the crew from the owner's house, and every racing day each member of the crew was given fruit, paid for by the owner. But perhaps the most generous gesture was the fact that each member of the crew who was prepared to join *Astra* for the following summer season received a retaining fee all winter. Thus, my sweetheart and I were able to furnish a small cottage and be married.'

The Cornish fishing winter of 1929 was one of the worst any fisherman in Looe could remember – and none of them, however skilful, dared put to sea until Christmas. Just before Christmas, however, A.J. received surprising news.

Sadly, Sir Mortimer had died, but in his will he had bequeathed £50

Left: *Our Daddy* at the Looe
quayside alongside *Emma*
(FY 299) in the 1930s

Below: *Our Daddy* and crew
during the good years just
after the Second World War

to each man who had crewed his beloved *Astra*. This unexpected gift saw A.J. and his bride through a desperate winter.

Then a further bonus arrived at the Pengellys' cottage in the form of a letter. It was from Captain Heard, who was to command Sir Thomas Lipton's new racing yacht, *Shamrock V*, which had been built to challenge for the America's Cup. Would A.J. like a berth on her? He promptly accepted, as did two other Looe men who had also been invited; and among the old sailing men of the town there is still an unshakeable belief that if ever the sailing skills of their fishermen were recognised it was on the day those letters came.

The crew of *Shamrock V* were paid £3 a week while in British waters, with the normal racing bonuses of £1 for first prize, 15 shillings (75p) for second, and 10 shillings (50p) for a start, and when they left for America it would be £5 a week, with a £50 bonus if they won the Cup. After competing successfully around the coasts of Britain, the yacht had to be sailed across the Atlantic for the Cup race. How she fared in the

Below: A.J. on board *Our Daddy*, both now semi-retired

race itself and why is described in another chapter of this book, but let
A.J.'s log tell the story of the arduous Atlantic crossing:

We semaphored to *Erin* [Sir Thomas's steam yacht which accompanied the
Shamrock V]. The ship is rolling badly. The *Erin* said we must sail on. . . . We look
for *Erin* in vain, but she seems to have vanished like the phantom ship of old. . . .
The wind is increasing. On go the hatches again, and the skylights are screwed
down. . . . The weather is so bad we set trysail, mizzen and jib. . . . These racing
yachts are build for speed under sail and so finely shaped at both ends that when they
plunge into the sea, the bow goes under and a lot of water comes aboard. Over each
quarter, and meeting in the middle. She's like a pendulum. I would much prefer to
be in a fishing boat. You can't look the squalls in the face to the windward for they
would cut your face. Everything is wet below: 'Somebody must have killed a cat!' All
hands are rather fed up. But by midnight the sea is smooth and the moon bright. . . .
   Heavy seas and the ship rolling like a barrel. I have never known a vessel like this.
We tried to have breakfast below, but the plates were sliding all over the floor. Each
man in turn at the wheel is lashed to the the mizzenmast. We have not been in our
quarters in the forecastle for three days and three nights. . . . On many days we have
been lucky to have anything cooked at all. By teatime we were down to tinned
pilchards, and as we were opening them, a sea broke and emptied down through a
skylight. Exit pilchards from tins! We scraped them from the floor. What a life!
Fishing on the mess deck. . . .

That Atlantic crossing took *Shamrock V* twenty-six days, but in the
early morning of 13 August 1930, in calm waters, she cut past the
Nantucket lightship and dropped anchor in New London Harbour.

After *Shamrock V*'s failure in the America's Cup, it was back to Looe
for A.J., crossing this time as a passenger aboard the Cunard liner
Caronia – a voyage more tranquil then his outward passage had been –
and back to another winter fishing season on *Our Daddy*. For the next
couple of years the mixture was as before: summers crewing the big
yachts and winters of Cornish fishing, punctuated by the familiar signs
of home that fishermen love, such as the 'Harvest of the Sea' celebration
in the local chapel, with decorations of nets, crab pots, lamps and
lifebuoys, and the singing of the old Sankey hymns. For A.J., however,
this satisfying calendar was not to last. Ill health prevented him from
accepting further invitations to crew aboard the 'gentlemen's yachts'
and he was back where he started – dependent upon fishing.

The mid-1930s were not the best time for it. No season seemed
destined to be a good one, and the Looe luggers voyaged to grounds far
from those they had ever thought their own. Eight and nine hours to the
seas off Devonshire they would venture before they set their sails and
shot their nets in search of herring, but even then the catches were
slender. There were a few good nights, of course – once, for example,

when they followed a cloud of seagulls and netted a catch that brought them £60 to share out for a night's work – but for the most part there was hardly a living to be made. During the whole of the 1936 winter season – from 12 November to 23 January – each member of the Pengelly boat crew earned a mere £19 15s (£19.75), and in the following year, from a mixed catch of pilchards, herring and mackerel, only £23 19s (£23.95).

The coming of the Second World War brought even more profound differences. Naval patrols shadowed the few fishing boats which ventured out, and in 1940 fishing was stopped altogether as the fear of invasion loomed. In 1941, however, when the restrictions were lifted and the smaller boats were permitted to work relatively close inshore, the fishermen were surprised at the rise in fishing stocks that had occurred. One morning, just off Looe Island, A.J. caught thirty-three turbot, and when *Our Daddy* was fitted with drift-nets to go to look for pilchards, the crew found, to their joy that they did not have to sail down to the tip of Cornwall, off Mount's Bay, but that the fish were just outside their own home harbour. It was the first time in twenty years that they had been able, in summer, to catch pilchards off Looe.

Throughout succeeding years similar changes, for vastly different reasons, have taken place in the industry that has been A.J's life. In 1948, for example, the size of the entire Cornish pilchard fleet increased to 160 boats, and the Looe fleet grew, too. Yet within a decade canners had gone out of business, and in the summers of 1959 and 1960, although only five boats were drift-netting out of Looe, they often brought into the port hundreds of stones of pilchards more than the canners could handle. The winter mackerel seasons improved for a time, but the summer pilchard fishing continued to decline. Whereas in 1948 there were 600 men and 160 boats engaged in it, in 1967 there were less than fifty men and fewer than ten boats.

Around this time, however, the summer brought to Looe the possibility of catching bigger fish: shark, which were swimming into the warmish Channel seas in increasing numbers. The *Our Daddy*, often with A.J. at the wheel, would set out in search of the new quarry. This time the fishermen aboard were not Looe men but holiday-makers out for a day's sport, and they used rods instead of nets. *Our Daddy* would leave a trail of 'rubby-dubby' (an evil-smelling mix of mashed-up rotting pilchards) to attract the shark; and in the evenings, as she rounded the harbour arm of Looe, she would land a cheery catch of anglers anxious that at least one photograph was taken of them with 'the shark that didn't get away'.

Today the adaptable Alfred John Pengelly and his hardy vessel are semi-retired. 'We shall probably end up, she and me,' he said, 'in a Maritime Museum. Mind you, she's got a lot of years left, you know. She's sixty-three, but in very good condition, so hopefully somebody will have her and look after her. I would actually like to see her go to a private person who could look after her and keep her for his own use. That's what I would finally like, I think.'

FURTHER READING

Living History Under Sail: Gaff Rig on the River Fal edited by John McDonald (Falmouth Working Boats Association, 1982).

Tall Ships: The World of Sail Training by Maldwin Drummond (Angus and Robertson, 1976).

Race Under Sail by Peter Hambly (Stanford Maritime, 1978).

The Tall Ships are Sailing by Holly Hollins (David & Charles, 1982).

Sailing Barges by Frank G. G. Carr (Conway Maritime Press, 1971).

Down Tops'l by Hervey Benham (Harrap, 1971).

Spritsail Barges of the Thames and Medway by Edgar J. March (David & Charles, 1970).

Enterprise to Endeavour: The J-Class Yachts by Ian Dear (Ian Allan, 1977).

Sacred Cowes by Anthony Heckstall-Smith (Anthony Blond, 1965).

Great Years in Yachting by John Nicholson (Nautical Publishing, 1970).

Sailing through Life by John Scott Hughes (Methuen, 1947).

Gaff Rig by John Leather (Adlard Coles, 1970).

Sailing Trawlers by Edgar J. March (David & Charles, 1953).

Sail: The Surviving Tradition by Robert Simper (Conway Maritime Press, 1984).

Victorian and Edwardian Yachting by Robert Simper (Batsford, 1984).

Gaff Sail by Robert Simper (Argus Books, 1979).

The Sailing Boat by H. C. Folkard (Chapman & Hall, sixth edition 1906).

Yachting: The Badminton Library Volumes I and II (Ashford Press Publishing, 1985).

Good Night Irene by Leslie Morrish (February Press, 1985).

Deep Water Sail by Harold Underhill (Brown, Son & Ferguson, Glasgow, 1952).

Schooner Captain by Hugh Shaw (D. Bradford Barton, Truro, 1972).

The Last of the Sailing Coasters by Edmund Eglinton (HMSO, 1982).

Schooner Man by Captain Richard England (Hollis & Carter, 1981).

Oh, For a Fisherman's Life: An Autobiography by Alfred John Pengelly BEM (Glasney Press, Falmouth, 1979).

USEFUL ADDRESSES

Association of Sea Training Organisations
c/o Royal Yachting Association
Victoria Way
Woking, Surrey GU21 1EQ

Thames Barge Sailing Club
c/o National Maritime Museum
Park Row, Greenwich
London SE10 9NF

Society for Spritsail Barge Research
c/o Hon Sec, 9 Camborne Road
Ipswich, Suffolk IP5 7JP

Dolphin Sailing Barge Museum
Crown Quay Lane
Sittingbourne, Kent

Old Gaffers Association
Bill Brown, Membership Secretary
Wheal Cock, Porkellis
Helston, Cornwall TR13 0JS

Irene Sailing Society
Bishops Lodge, Oakley Green
Windsor, Berkshire SL4 5UL

Exeter Maritime Museum
The Quay
Exeter, Devon EX2 4AN

PICTURE CREDITS

Photographs reproduced by courtesy of the following:
BARNABY'S PICTURE LIBRARY pages 48 & 118; BBC HULTON PICTURE LIBRARY pages 43 & 60; BEKEN OF COWES page 65; JANKA BIELAK pages 26 & 29; DIE BILDSTELLE DER MARINE page 23; COLLORYAN page 117; TREVOR DAVIES page 120; IAN DEAR pages 68, 73, 76, 78, 81 & 151; PETER FERGUSON COLLECTION pages 45 & 58; PETER HAWES pages 55, 57, 63, 89 & 122; BRIAN HAWKINS pages 11, 12 & 143; TOM JARRATT page 113; JAMES MATTHEWS JOYCE pages 145 & 154; TOM LAWLOR pages 37 & 39; LESLIE MORRISH page 132; NATIONAL MARITIME MUSEUM, GREENWICH pages 15, 130, 147 & 153; A. J. PENGELLY page 148; RADIO TIMES pages 32 & 35; WILLIAM G. ROWNTREE pages 108 & 110; NICK SHIPLEY page 141; ROBERT SIMPER pages 19, 84, 95, 96 & 98.